TOP-DECK TRAVEL
A HISTORY OF BRITAIN'S OPEN-TOP BUSES

PHILIP C. MILES

The History Press

I would like to dedicate this book to my dear Mother in loving memory.

First published 2009

The History Press
The Mill, Brimscombe Port
Stroud, Gloucestershire, GL5 2QG
www.thehistorypress.co.uk

ISBN 978 0 7524 5137 4

Typesetting and origination by The History Press
Printed in Great Britain

CONTENTS

ACKNOWLEDGEMENTS

I would like to thank the following people for helping me with this book: Arriva; The Original London Sightseeing Tour; The Big Bus Company, London; Steve White; Geoff Mills and Pete Shipp. I would also like to thank the following people for allowing me to use their photographs: Dick Gilbert; Arriva London; Timebus; Robert F. Mack; C. Carter; David Longbottom; Lancaster City Transport; John H. Meredith; Steve White; Andrew Jarosz; Geoff Mills; The Big Bus Company, London; Essex Bus Enthusiasts' Group; M&D and East Kent Bus Club; Isle of Man Transport; Southdown Enthusiasts' Club; W. J. Haynes; Eric Surfleet; Roy Marshall; C. Warren; L.W. Rowe; D. Clark; S.J. Butler; Malcolm King; Ribble Enthusiasts' Club; Huddersfield Passenger Transport Group.

INTRODUCTION

My first experience of riding on an open-top bus was in the summer of 1972 when I visited the Isle of Wight. The excitement of seeing Bristol Loddekas and a Bristol K for the first time still touches me. I was only used to seeing AECs, Leyland Atlanteans and Daimler Fleetlines in my native City of Hull and what struck me about these new types of buses was that they didn't have roofs. Staying at Shanklin, I was in the ideal location to observe the open-top buses operating from here to Sandown Zoo.

Some thirty-five years later I still get the same thrill as I did then. I remember Southern Vectis was just starting to paint its buses from their original Tilling's green and cream to the National Bus Co. green and white livery – although the open-top Bristol K remained mainly cream. The thrill of going upstairs onto the top deck as the bus was travelling down the steep hill from Shanklin promenade into town, the feel of the wind blowing in my face! I felt I could touch the beautiful thatched cottages.

A few years later I visited Teignmouth in Devon and remember catching the open-top bus to Torquay on a service usually operated by Bristol VRT convertible open-top buses, but on this rare occasion an open-top Leyland Atlantean was operating the service. These vehicles were painted in the then National Bus Co. standard open-top livery.

Since then I have travelled on many open-top buses up and down the country, and I never get tired of travelling on top. Perhaps one of the most exciting open-top bus rides I ever took was in the Lake District. The bus travelled at speed through some of the most beautiful scenery in the United Kingdom. This occurred some years ago when I was staying in Morecambe where, incidentally, open-top buses are also operated up and down the promenade. One day I drove to Bowness and caught the open-top bus 599 to Grasmere. At the time these buses were operated by Stagecoach and painted in an attractive green and cream livery.

In this book I have tried to capture the many different types of buses used as open-top buses, from half cab, rear entrance AEC Regents, Guy Arabs and Leyland Titans and the later Leyland Atlanteans, Daimler Fleetlines and Bristol VRTs to the modern buses of today. Not to mention the fact that bus operators often decided to simply take the roof off an old bus, and in this form the bus would give several more years of service. Other bus operators purchased specially adapted buses which they could fit with roofs during the winter months, then, during the summer months, have the roof and upper-deck windows removed and stored away.

Although I have tried to capture the many types of open-top buses operating in this county, it is an impossible task to include every vehicle and every bus operator running them. I apologise for any open-top buses or operators which have not been remembered in this book.

Philip C. Miles
Kingston upon Hull

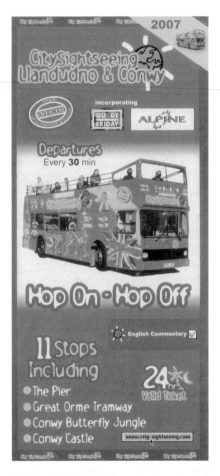

Attractive leaflets help to promote open-top bus services. These two leaflets show to good effect what can be achieved. They are cheerful and contain all the information needed for would-be passengers, such as running times, a well-detailed map and fares.

1

EARLY DOUBLE-DECK BUSES

Our story of the open-top double-deck bus begins over a hundred years ago. This unique vehicle first made its appearance in England as early as 1904, the year that Milnes-Daimler displayed a 24hp thirty-four-seat double-deck bus at the Crystal Palace Motor Car Show. Although basic by today's standards, this marks the beginning of something great. The driver sat behind the engine in the open, but the roof from the lower saloon was extended forwards over the driver to form a canopy. The enclosed lower-deck had inward-facing seats for sixteen passengers. An open staircase at the rear of the bus allowed access to the upper-deck where nine forward-facing seats capable of seating eighteen passengers were to be found.

The Milnes-Daimler double-deck bus was a success story, and many of the pioneer bus operators purchased these vehicles. The design was basic, based on the horse bus, but effective – providing the basis for double-deck buses for the next twenty-five years.

Bus operators in London were quick to purchase the new double-deck bus, with two well-known operators, Thomas Tilling Ltd and Birch Bros Ltd, operating them in 1904. However, rivals to the Milnes-Daimler were soon born. In 1905 London General Omnibus Co. Ltd and London Road Car Co. Ltd purchased many Bussings double-deck buses, supplied through Straker and Squire Engineers, who later built the buses under licence. Leyland introduced a double-deck vehicle in 1905. London & Suburban Omnibus Co. also purchased a number of these vehicles. The English bus manufacturers, Leyland, Dennis, Daimler and AEC, were quick to bring out their own double-deck models.

Leyland had been building steam buses for a number of years. In 1904 they built an experimental lorry chassis which soon went into production as it was suitable for a double-deck bus and London & Suburban Omnibus Co. placed an order for it. This

The steam omnibus was a rare model indeed. This is the original Clarkson steam bus, built in Chelmsford as early as 1903 and registered F233. (Essex Bus Enthusiasts' Group)

company, with investment from Leyland, became London Central Co., and built up a large Leyland fleet before selling out to London General in 1912. Other bus companies also purchased the Leyland double-deck bus.

The most popular double-deck buses were the G-type series, and later the forward control version, the SG series. Chocolate Express Co. of London purchased LB models, which were similar to the G7 but built to meet the Metropolitan Police requirements of the time. AEC Co. built sixty-one experimental 'X'-type chassis for double-deck buses in 1909. However, the 'B'-type was perhaps the most popular double-deck bus, especially in London. About 3,000 were in operation in the capital by mid-1914. A large number of AEC 'B'-types were commandeered at the beginning of the First World War, serving as troop carriers in France and Belgium. Daimler exhibited a purpose-built double-deck bus with the driver sitting to the right of the engine, behind a much smaller bonnet compared with other buses of the time. In 1910 the 'KPL' model was built. Tramways

(MET) Omnibus Co. ordered 350 Daimler double-deck buses, which entered service in 1912. The Daimler was very similar in design to the AEC 'B' model operated by London General Omnibus Co.

After the end of the war, in 1919, LGOC introduced the AEC 'K'-type to the fleet. The 'K'-type, unlike the 'B'-type, had forward control with the driver being situated besides the engine. The new model was larger and could carry up to forty-six passengers. A total of 1,157 models were produced.

A new model was introduced in 1922: the AEC 'S'-type, with seating for fifty-four passengers. A year later the AEC 'NS'-type was introduced. Bristol was slow in building double-deck buses, and it was not until 1923 that the first nine double-deck four-tonners were purchased by Kingston upon Hull Corporation Tramways, with its Dick Kerr fifty-three-seat bodywork, whilst Guy, another latecomer to the double-deck market, introduced its first double-deck model in 1926 – a six-wheel vehicle.

By the mid- to late 1920s few operators were still purchasing new open-top double-deck buses. Morecambe Corporation was one such exception, continuing to purchase new Guy FBX open-top double-deck buses, whilst Hastings & District added open-top Guy BTX six-wheeler trolleybuses to their fleet in 1928.

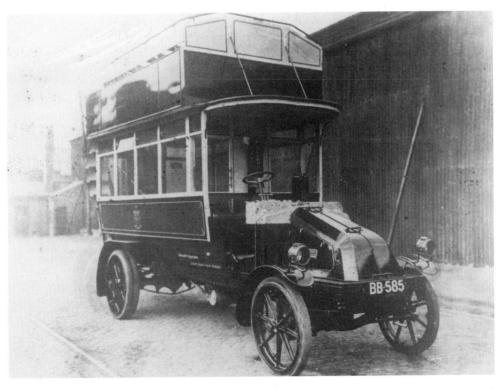

Newcastle Corporation Tramways purchased its first motorbuses in 1912. These were registered BB585-588 and were Tilling Stevens TDA1s with open-top thirty-four-seat bodywork. These vehicles were used for a tramway extension service between Whorlton church and Fenham Barracks. BB585, the first of the batch, is seen here. (Philip C. Miles collection)

The National Omnibus & Transport fleet of Essex operated No.2152, an AEC 'Y'. The 'Y'-type was a popular chassis for double-deck buses in the early 1920s. (Essex Bus Enthusiasts' Group)

The much larger 'S'-type was more powerful than its predecessor, the 'K'-type. Introduced in 1922, it was a fifty-four-seat vehicle. In this photograph of S454, now preserved, it shows the open staircase and open upper-deck as well as the solid tyres. (Philip C. Miles collection)

Silver Queen Motor Omnibus Co. Ltd operated this Leyland G (NO6623), with open staircase, in the Clackton area. This company was acquired by newly formed Eastern National Co. in September 1931. (Essex Bus Enthusiasts' Group)

This Halford double-deck open-top bus was once in the fleet of the Maidstone, Clapham, Gravesend and District Motor Services. New in 1908, it is thought to be registered D3449. It is seen here at Rose Yard in Mews, Maidstone. (The M&D and East Kent Bus Club)

Perhaps the most popular and best-known early double-deck bus was the AEC 'B'-type, powered by a 30hp four-cylinder petrol engine with seating for thirty-four passengers. Over 3,000 of this model were produced between 1910 and 1920. When the First World War broke out, many of the London General fleet of 'B'-types were commandeered by the War Department to carry troops to the battlefields of France and Belgium. (Philip C. Miles collection)

In 1915 the Maidstone & District Motor Services purchased this Straker Squire 400hp bus with a Tillings body. Two Straker Squire double-deck buses were purchased that year: KT 6882, with a Dodson open-top body, and KT 6415, shown here displaying a board for one of the original routes operated by the company. (M&D and East Kent Bus Club)

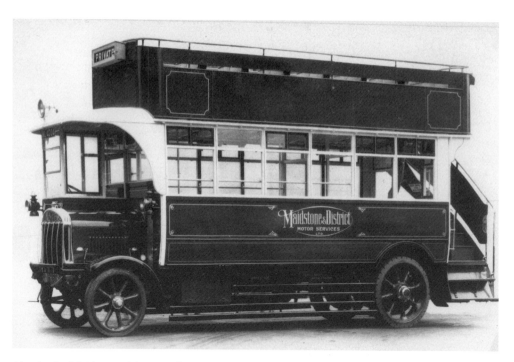

Also in the Maidstone & District fleet is No.53 (KL 4204), a Tilling Stevens TS6 petrol/electric bus with a Tillings fifty-one-seat open-top body, purchased in 1925. (M&D and East Kent Bus Club)

Douglas Corporation Tramways No.8 (MN 1880), a 1922 Tilling Stevens TS3A with a Tilling forty-nine-seat body. The management and crew pose proudly with their new bus. (Isle of Man Transport)

A few years later buses were fitted with pneumatic tyres, but still had an open staircase and open-top. Purchased by Morecambe Corporation, this Guy FBX was new in 1926/27. The driver was under cover. This vehicle was numbered 6 (TD 7098) and is a fifty-three-seater. (C. Carter)

2

LONDON AND THE SOUTH COAST

In 1972 London saw the return of open-top buses when London Transport hired five Guy Arab IIIs with Park Royal bodywork from East Kent. These buses were new in 1951, and were converted to open-tops in the 1960s. These were operated on sightseeing tours of London, visiting the attractions for a fare of 65*p*.

In 1975, due to the success of the open-top buses on the Round London Sightseeing Tour, preservationist and London bus enthusiast Prince Marshall purchased seven ex-Midland Red BMMO D9s, numbered OM1-7, from what was then a small company named Ensign of Grays. They were converted to open-top and operated on the Round London Sightseeing Tour in full London Transport livery, with exclusive advertising for Johnny Walker whisky. The tour of the capital lasted for about two hours, with no stopping points. The D9s had seating for seventy-two passengers with forty of those able to be seated on the upper-deck. These vehicles were hired for three years, although a number operated for some time after that on a short-lived 74Z shuttle service operating between Regent's Park Zoo and Baker Street Station. The Round London Sightseeing Tour's open-top buses were such a success that London Transport purchased its own vehicles to work this tour. In 1977 seven twelve-year-old Daimler Fleetlines with Alexander convertible open-top bodies were purchased from Bournemouth Corporation Transport. London Transport numbered these vehicles DMO1-7. Unfortunately, these were short-lived, being withdrawn from the tour and sold between 1979 and 1980. Now deregulated, from October 1980 a number of London Transport DMS-class buses were sold to the Ensign dealership, who in return sold them to other companies. Some were sub-contracted to operate the Round London Sightseeing Tour, while others found their way to competitors.

Ensign, who had a stake in London Pride, then hired buses back to London Transport. A large number of DMSs were converted to open-top and operated by several companies, all competing for the same passengers. London Transport formed a new division, London Coaches. In 1986 they transferred fifty AEC Routemasters to the new company to operate the Round London Sightseeing Tour. These were converted to open-top buses or convertible open-top buses. With the standard Routemaster able to carry only thirty-six passengers upstairs, London Coaches lengthened a number of standard RMs (Routemasters) by adding a single bay using material from previously scrapped Routemasters. These vehicles became known as ERMs (extended Routemasters) which were 32ft 6in long.

Arriva bought the sightseeing business from London Coaches in 1998. The Original London Sightseeing Tour, as it was called, contained a large assortment of vehicles including lengthened Routemasters, standard length Routemasters, Metroliner coaches, Olympians and Metrobuses. Later converts to open-tops were DAF DB250s, with Plaxton President bodywork. In 2001 Arriva added tri-axle Metrobuses purchased from New World First Bus, Hong Kong, to their fleet.These large vehicles can carry seventy-five passengers on the upper-deck alone. They also operated the new Spanish-built Ayats on Volvo B7L chassis. In 2007 the Original Tour took delivery of ten new Volvo B7Tls with East Lancs Visionaire open-top bodies.

A new open-top company was formed in 1991. This was The Big Bus Co., beginning with only two buses. The company grew and is now the largest operator of open-top buses in the capital, covering two main tourist routes: a red tour which operates every twenty to thirty minutes, and the blue tour which also runs every twenty to thirty minutes. A green link across London covers all the best sights of the capital, providing live commentary in eight different languages. The Big Bus Co. was also the first operator to offer a free river cruise

The Big Bus Co. have operated ex-London Transport Leyland Titan TNLXB2RRs, Bristol VRTs, Leyland Fleetlines, Leyland Atlanteans, as well as a 1959 Park Royal-bodied AEC Regent V. New buses include Metrobuses with Metro Cammell-Weymann bodies, either partially open or fully open sixty-one or forty-one-seat buses, purchased from New World First, Hong Kong. Several other operators have operated open-top tours of London.

Another early operator of a tour around London was London Sightseeing Tours Ltd. This company operated ex-London Transport Daimlers on a guided tour lasting between one and a half hours to two hours. London Pride was another operator who operated Metrobuses as well as Metroliner coaches on the Round London Sightseeing Tour.

The sunnier and much warmer south coast with its many holiday resorts is a haven for tourists, and therefore for open-top buses. East Kent Road Car began operating open-top buses in several coastal resorts in 1959. In that year two open-top bus services were also introduced at Thanet. A number of utility Guy Arabs were converted for use on these services. These two routes were expanded and modified over the years, until the two services were finally linked, operating around a sixteen-mile area on the Isle of Thanet, along the coastline from Pegwell Bay, Hoverport, to Minnis Bay. A second open-top bus service was introduced in 1962 at Herme Bay, service 45, whilst a third open-top bus service was introduced between Folkestone and Dover as service 1. It later expanded into an hourly service between St Mary's Bay and Ashford Airport to Dover.

Also in Kent, the historical town of Hastings was once served by Maidstone & District Motor Services, who had for many years operated open-top single-deck buses on a tour of the town, starting at the Old Fishmarket. Dennis Aces were originally used, until they were replaced by three Beadle-bodied AEC Regals, before converting to open-top AEC Reliances with Weymann bodywork

Hastings Tramways Co. operated an open-top trolleybus (No.3A), a 1928 Guy BTX60 with a Dodson fifty-seven-seat open-top deck and staircase. This company was acquired by Maidstone & District in 1957. In 1960 No.3A was given a Commer TS3 diesel engine and underwent other modifications to enable it to carry on the seafront service at Hastings.

In Eastbourne the use of open-top buses operating along the seafront to Beachy Head goes back many years. An agreement was reached between Southdown Motor Services and Eastbourne Corporation Transport which only allowed the corporation's buses to operate within the town limits.

The area around Brighton was serviced by a number of operators. These were Brighton, Hove & District, Southdown Motor Services and Brighton Corporation Transport. Southdown Motor Services was an early user of open-top buses on summer bus routes around the seaside, operating route 27, Brighton to Devil's Dyke, and service 31F, operating between Brighton and Worthing, using vehicles from their final batch of 1929 Leyland Titans.

Brighton, Hove & District also operated AEC Regents and Bristol Lodekkas fitted with removable top-deck covers on service 17, operating between Rottingdean and Portslade. Southdown Motor Services also operated service 102 between Arundel and Devil's Dyke, a thirty-four-mile journey taking an hour to complete, with superb views of the Sussex countryside en route. Southdown is well known for its smart convertible Northern Counties Leyland Titan PD3s, but they also operated Guy Arabs, built in 1944 and converted to open-tops in 1957. In later years Southdown operated dual-doorway Bristol VRTs in standard NBC leaf green liveries. In 1979 Brighton Corporation Transport took over the open-top service 17 from Hove to Saltdean. For this service Brighton Transport converted four front-entrance Leyland Titan PD3/4s with MCW bodies, numbers 32-35, to open-tops in 1968.

Southdown operated service 97, a seafront service starting from the old Royal Parade bus garage via the steep hairpin bends to the top of Beachy Head, giving fantastic views and many a nail-biting moment as the Guy Arabs and later the Northern Counties-bodied Leyland Titans climbed the steep hills. Originally, only single-deck buses could operate the seafront service. With this in mind Southdown Motor Services purchased two six-wheel Leyland Tiger TS6Ts with Short Bros forty-seat bodies. These vehicles had folding roofs so the passengers could enjoy the fresh air. Also operated by Southdown was the 197 onward to Birling Gap, returning via East Dean and the town centre. Eastbourne Corporation Transport also operated the seafront service, with the early open-top service beginning at the railway station, reaching the seafront at the Redoubt and then running along the full length of the parade, past the pier to the foot of Beachy Head. The return route went via Meads. The service, now operational for over fifty years, was later numbered service 6, but is now numbered service 3 and operates to the top of Beachy Head.

Eastbourne Corporation Transport prefixed all their open-top buses between 1949 and 1963 with the words 'The White', except for numbers 94 and 95 where the word 'The' was omitted. Numbers 6-10 were the last vehicles to be named after the conversion to open-tops in 1954 (No.10 was converted to open-top in 1956) until 1985.

64. JK 1239 1930 Leyland TD1 Leyland named *The White Knight*
75. JK 1814 1931 Leyland TD1 (with East Lancs body added in 1942) named *The White King*
77. JK 2235 1932 Leyland TD2 Leyland named *The White Princess*
78. JK 2236 1932 Leyland TD2 Leyland named *The White Queen*
79. JK 2337 1932 Leyland TD2 Leyland named *The White Rabbit*
80. JK 2338 1932 Leyland TD2 Leyland named *The White Lady*
94. JK 5604 1936 AEC Regent Leyland named *White Heather*
95. JK 5605 1936 AEC Regent Leyland named *White Ensign*
96. JK 5606 1936 AEC Regent Leyland named *The White King*
6. JK 7427 1938 AEC Regent Northern Counties named *The White Princess*
7. JK 7428 1938 AEC Regent Northern Counties named *The White Rabbit*
8. JK 7429 1938 AEC Regent Northern Counties named *The White Lady*
9. JK 7430 1938 AEC Regent Northern Counties named *The White Queen*
10 JK 7431 1938 AEC Regent Northern Counties named *The White Knight*
65. LDX 75G 1968 Leyland Atlantean ECW named *Eastbourne King*
66. LDX 74G 1968 Leyland Atlantean ECW named *Eastbourne Queen*

Brighton & Hove, successor to Southdown Motor Services, operated convertible open-top Dennis Tridents, as well as purchasing two Scania N94UD Omnidekkas with East Lancs CO47/32F bodies, numbered 617 and 618, and named *Douglas Reeve* and *Danny Sheldon* respectively. They have been facilitated to carry one wheelchair each.

Portsmouth, Plymouth and Southampton Transports have all operated open-top buses at one time or another. Plymouth City Transport converted a Leyland Titan PD2/12 into an open-top and operated this on the route 38 circular from the city centre to the seafront. This vehicle was named after the city's famous seaman, Sir Francis Drake. A later convert to open-top was No.458, a 1962 Leyland Atlantean with Metro Cammell bodywork, used on service 54 between the City Centre, the Hoe and the Barbican. Portsmouth Corporation Transport converted four 1935 Leyland Titan TD4s with English Electric bodies to open-top between 1953 and 1955. For a service between Clarence Pier and Hayling Ferry, six Leyland Titan PD2/12s with Metro Cammell bodies, numbered 1-6, new in 1956, were also converted to open-top. Later Metro Cammell-bodied Leyland Atlanteans were decapitated to continue the seafront service 25. Southampton Corporation Transport converted two Guy Arab IIIs with Park Royal bodies into open-tops to operate tours of the docks. Provincial converted an ex-City of Oxford Motor Service AEC Regent No.19 into open-top in 1951. A year later the company converted a Bristol K5G, No.54, with a Park Royal utility body. Other buses to convert to open-top were Guy's numbers 18 and 56 in 1956. A third bus was re-bodied in 1956 by Readings, and fitted with a detachable roof, although it seems that this vehicle kept its roof until withdrawn, and was not used as an open-top bus. Nevertheless, these open-top buses were used during the summer season on routes to Stokes Bay and Lee-on-Solent, although they sometimes made rare appearances on the 1 and 3 inland routes. After de-regulation the new company became known as People's

Provincial, and also operated open-top buses in the 1990s on the Southsea seafront, a service formerly operated by Portsmouth City Transport. People's Provincial operated ex-Southdown Motor Services Queen Mary fully fronted Leyland Titans, ex-Bournemouth Corporation Daimler Fleetlines and Bristol VRTs on this service. Solent Blue currently uses convertible open-top East Lancs Myllennium Yyking Volvo B7Tls. These vehicles, which were transferred from Wilts & Dorset, have bicycle trailers fitted which are used on the New Forest tour. Solent Blue also operates open-top buses on the dock tour.

Devon General was once the main operator in the Torbay area, operating open-top services on the Babbacombe, Torquay and Paignton services. The service from Dawlish Warren via Teignmouth to Torquay on the 137 service took an hour, with superb coastal views, whilst another service, the 122 starting at Babbacombe via Torquay, runs southwards via Paignton and Brixham to Kingswear. A feature of the Devon General open-top buses were their unusual names, dating back to 1919. This carried on with the naming of nine convertible Leyland Atlantean PDR1/1s with Metro Cammell bodies in 1961. These were all named after famous Elizabethan seamen. Known collectively as the 'Sea Dog' class, they were numbered and named:

925. *Admiral Blake*
926. *Sir Francis Drake*
927. *Martin Frobisher*
928 *Sir Humphrey Gilbery*
929. *Sir Richard Grenville*

930. *Sir John Hawkins*
931. *Sir Thomas Howard*
932. *Earl Howe*
933. *Sir Walter Raleigh*

In 1977 eleven Bristol VRTSL3-6LXBs with ECW bodies entered the fleet. All eleven of these vehicles are named after famous warships and were numbered and named:

934. *Golden Hind*, later renamed *Sir Thomas Hardy*
935. *Triumph*
936. *Revenge*
937. *Victory*
938. *Warspite*
939. *Renown*
940. *Invincible*
941. *Illustrious*
942. *Hermes*, later renamed *Lawrence of Arabia*
943. *Ark Royal*
944. *Vanguard*

Not all of these vehicles operated in the Devon General fleet: 937, 941, 942 and 944 operated in the Western National fleet, although they retained the poppy red livery of the former. No.934 was operated by Southern National in the Falmouth area. No.942 joined the Southern National fleet in 1983 and was painted into NBC green livery. Over the years some of vehicles have changed names, for example 935, when owned by Bayline, was renamed *Ark Royal*, whilst after privatisation the new Devon General fleet renamed 938 *Illustrious*. Stagecoach Devon, the new operator of Devon General, also named an ex-Stagecoach Coastline VRT with the old fleet No.937 *Invincible*. Southern National operated 555

(ATA555L), a 1973 Bristol VRT in the Weymouth area, and this vehicle was named *Sir Christopher Wren.* To add even more interest to the Devon fleet of open-top buses, Stagecoach Devon operated 992 (LRV 992), a Leyland Titan PD2/12 with a Metro Cammell body. New in 1956, this bus came from Thames Transit in 1997. During the spring of 2000 Stagecoach Devon operated ex-Stagecoach London Scania double-deck buses with Alexander bodywork, which were converted to open-tops to oust the remaining Bristol VRTs for use on the popular Torbay open-top bus routes. Across the Solent is the beautiful Isle of Wight, served by the Southern Vectis O.C. Once owned by Tilling Co. it then passed to the British Transport Commission in 1948 and National Bus Co. in 1969. The Isle of Wight, with its quaint thatched houses, beautiful bays and open-top buses, is still as popular today with tourists as it always was, and has a long tradition of open-top buses. Many of the older buses used here were converted to open-top after arriving from mainland bus operators including Hants & Dorset, Bristol O.C. and Brighton, Hove & District, giving many more years of service in their new location. Later Southern Vectis's own Bristol Lodekkas were converted to open-top. The open-top services which now operated were: No.7 between Ryde and Seaview, No.42 from Yarmouth to Alum Bay, No.44 from Sandown Zoo to Shanklin Esplanade – where it became No.45 to Vetnor via Shanklin Bus Station – and No.47 from Sandown Zoo to Shanklin Bus Station and Vetnor. At one time Southern Vectis operated the oldest bus in regular service: No.702 (CDL 899) – renumbered 502 in 1984. New in 1939, this Bristol K5G was also converted to open-top. Seen in a number of liveries over the years, none beat its original cream livery with green relief lining. Later, in 1979, Bristol VRT convertibles were purchased from Hants & Dorset. Converted Olympians now operate the service.

For many years Bournemouth operated open-top buses as well as being one of the few operators to use open-top trolleybuses. Many thousands of passengers in the summer would have travelled on Bournemouth's service 12, operating along the cliffs from Sandbanks to Christchurch, stopping at Boscombe Pier, Bournemouth Pier, Branksome Chine and Canford Cliffs. Over the years various types of buses have been converted to open-top, including the fully fronted 1939 Weymann-bodied Leyland Titan TD5s. These vehicles had a sliding roof fitted when new but were converted to open-top in 1958. Bournemouth Corporation Transport converted 1936 Sunbeam MS2 trolleybuses with Park Royal bodies into open-tops in 1958, giving nearly thirty years of service in Bournemouth. In 1965 Bournemouth Corporation Transport took delivery of numbers 180-189, Weymann-bodied Daimler Fleetlines convertible to open-top. These vehicles were named after counties in England:

180. *Lancashire*
181. *Yorkshire*
182. *Warwickshire*
183. *Staffordshire*
184. *Cheshire*
185. *Dorset*
186. *Hampshire*
187. *Durham*
188. *Northumberland*
189. *Surrey*

Photographed back in London Transport days, fifty AEC Routemasters were transferred to the newly formed London Coaches division to operate the Round London Sightseeing Tour. Several were converted to open-top, including RM925 (WLT 925) which was converted to this style in 1986. (Philip C. Miles collection)

Blue Triangle operated this ex-London Transport Daimler Fleetline CRL6 with a Park Royal seventy-one-seat converted open-top body. New in 1975 as No.DM1110, GHV 110N is seen here on a sightseeing tour of London. Note the hand-written notice in the side of the window. (Philip C. Miles collection)

Above: A more unusual open-top bus to operate on the London Sightseeing Tour is this RT, operated by London Pride. Former London Transport RT 4196 (LYF 228) is photographed at Tower Hill. (Geoff Mills)

Opposite: London Pride was operating this MCW Metroliner DR130/3 on sightseeing tours of London. It was new to Shamrock & Rambler Coaches Ltd as their 3112 (A112 KFX), and later renumbered 112. The large seating capacity of fifty-seven upstairs is an ideal choice for a tour of London. (Philip C. Miles collection)

Nine new Daimler and Leyland Fleetlines with Alexander Als, convertible to open-top bodies, were added to the fleet in 1976 and 1978. The most recent convertible open-top buses operated by Yellowbuses are Volvo B7TLs with East Lancs Vyking bodies, delivered in 2002. To celebrate 100 years of service, in 2002 No.431 was painted in a special gold and blue livery and lettered 'Bournemouth Transport Centenary 1902-2002'. Also based at Bournemouth Bus Station, Hants & Dorset operated fully fronted open-top Bristol Ks between Bournemouth Square and Sandbanks. Wilts & Dorset now operate the Swanage route and the Lymington and Poole areas. The modern open-top buses used by Wilts & Dorset include Volvo B7Tls with East Lancs Myllennium Vyking bodies, DAF DB250 with Northern Counties Palatine II bodies and Leyland Olympians with ECW or Roe bodywork.

During the summer of 2008 the open-top bus service in Bournemouth was operated not by Transdev Yellowbuses but by Totally Transport, based in Blackpool, the Lancastrian Transport Trust community interest company, along with preservationist Eric Stobart, using a varied selection of vehicles which included an ex-Crosville VRT numbered 901, an Alexander-bodied Bristol VRT, new to Cardiff City Transport, and a former Bournemouth Corporation Transport Daimler Fleetline which was converted to have a partially open-top. These vehicles were painted in a smart custard and plum livery.

Now with Arriva, the former London Transport RM1864 (864 DYE) is a standard un-lengthened AEC Routemaster converted to open-top for the Original Tour of London. The half cab AEC Routemasters looks superb in their new form. (Steve White)

A rare and unusual sight on the streets of London, this Bristol VRT with an ECW body which has been partially converted to open-top is seen on the Original London Sightseeing Tour. New to East Midland Motor Services as No.184 (AET 184T) in 1978, it is a VRTSL/6LXB model with seating for seventy-five. (Steve White)

Arriva was operating OA341 (J341 BSH), a Leyland Olympian with an Alexander dual-doorway body converted to partially open-top. OA341 is seen here on the Original London Sightseeing Tour. (Philip C. Miles collection)

Timebus operates two open-top AEC Routemasters. One of the two shown here is RM479 (WSJ 737), previously registered WLT479 when owned by London Transport. Timebus operates these buses on private hire, for weddings and film shoots. RM479 is seen with wedding ribbon and a bouquet on the occasion of David and Miranda's wedding (see destination board). (Timebus)

New to the New World Firstbus Hong Kong fleet in 1988 was the The Big Bus Co. No.ML20 (B20 DMS). These large Metrobuses with MCW bodies can carry sixty-one passengers on the top deck, which is useful in carrying large numbers of tourists on sightseeing tours of London. They also seat a further thirty-nine passengers downstairs. (The Big Bus Co.)

Opposite above: Arriva, the Original London Sightseeing Tour operator, also operates ex-New World Firstbus Hong Kong Metrobuses. These tri-axled Metrobuses with rebuilt partial open-top bodies seating seventy-five passengers on the upper-deck and a further thirty-three downstairs. This one is numbered EMB768 (E768 JAR) and was new in 1987. It was acquired for the London Sightseeing Tour in 2001. (Philip C. Miles collection)

Opposite below: The newest open-top double-deck buses for Arriva's Original London Sightseeing Tour are these Volvo B7Ls with Spanish-built Ayats O51/24F bodies. The first of this batch is VLV601 (LX05 GEJ), photographed here before entering service. (Arriva London)

Converted for the coastal service to Palm Bay is East Kent Road Car FFN380. New in 1951, this is a Guy Arab III 6LW with a Park Royal H30/26R body. It was converted to open-top in 1962. (Photograph by J.T. Wilson/Southdown Enthusiasts' Club)

Maidstone & District 297 (FKO 227) was a 1939 Leyland Titan TD5 with a Weymann H24/24R body. Seen here with its old fleet number, it was renumbered OT3 in 1958. (W.J. Haynes/Southdown Enthusiasts' Club)

Holidaymakers enjoy the fresh air on board BJG 472, on their way to Palm Bay. East Kent Road Car operated this 1945 Guy Arab II. The Weymann fifty-six-seat body has been cut down to an open-top. It was converted for the seafront service in 1959, and remained in use until it was withdrawn in 1969, by then twenty-four years old. (Philip C. Miles collection)

Maidstone & District Motor Services converted this 1946 Bristol K6A with a Weymann fifty-six-seat body to open-top in 1957. No.180 (HKL 863) was renumbered OT8 in the same year. (The M&D & East Kent Enthusiasts' Club)

A once familiar sight in Hastings, this open-top single-deck bus was used on the Round the Town Tour. For this purpose Maidstone & District converted three attractive Beadle-bodied AEC Regals to open-tops. No.SO9 (HKL 819) is seen here, renumbered OR1 after its conversion in 1958. (Eric Surfleet collection/Southdown Enthusiasts' Club)

A full load of passengers are ready to enjoy the sights from this Southdown Motor Services 121 (GUF121), a 1944 Guy Arab II 6LW with a Northern Counties open-top fifty-six-seat body. It was converted to open-top in 1957. 121 is about to set off from Brighton (Pool Valley Bus Station) to Devil's Dyke. (Eric Surfleet/Southdown Enthusiasts' Club)

Open-top trolleybuses are a rarity. However, Hastings & District Tramways operated eight Guy BTXs with Dodson bodies. These vehicles dated from the opening of the trolleybus system in 1928, and this example is in disguise as 'Happy Harold', No.3A (DY 4695). (Philip C. Miles collection)

New in 1932, this Eastbourne Corporation Transport Leyland Titan TD2 No.80 (JK 2338) with a Leyland H24/24R body was rebuilt in the corporation workshops in 1949 to open-top form, re-seated to O28/24R. No.80 was named *The White Lady*. (Eric Surfleet/Southdown Enthusiasts' Club)

With the old open-top buses dating from the 1930s coming to the end of their life, Eastbourne Corporation Transport decided to convert a number of post-war PD1s to open-top. Vehicles 13, 14, 6 and 18 were all PD1s with attractive East Lancs H28/24R bodywork, and were new in 1946. These buses were converted to open-top in 1961. Seen in this photograph is No.16 (JK 9114). These open-top buses were the first such vehicles to be fitted with an upper-deck front windscreen. (Philip C. Miles collection)

Brighton, Hove & District 6200 (GN6200) is a 1935 AEC Regent with a Dodson fifty-two-seat body. No.6200 was converted to open-top in 1936 and awaits passengers on the open-top service 17, operating between Portslade and Rottingdean, passing Hove Lagoon, the piers and the well-known Black Rock en route. (Roy Marshall/Southdown Enthusiasts' Club)

Also seen on the open-top service 17, and new in 1935, is Brighton, Hove & District 6286 (GW 6286), another AEC Regent but with a Tilling H27/25R body. It was converted to open-top by the company in 1946. The young boy in the photograph seems more interested in the test match latest then the AEC Regent. (Eric Sunfleet/Southdown Enthusiasts' Club)

In 1940 Brighton, Hove & District purchased a large number of Bristol K5Gs with ECW H30/26R bodies. These were numbered 6348-62. A number of these were converted to open-top between 1951 and 1955, including 6358 (CAP 230), renumbered 358 in 1955. The vehicle in this photograph was converted to open-top in 1951. (Southdown Enthusiasts' Club)

A later Bristol K5G to be converted to open-top for use on the No.17 seafront service is Brighton, Hove & District 5994 (EHY 581) with an ECW H30/26R body. New to Bristol Tramways as No.C3119 in 1938, it was acquired by Brighton, Hove & District in 1955 and converted to open-top in the same year. Few seats remain vacant as the renumbered 994 heads towards Rottingdean. (Southdown Enthusiasts' Club)

Brighton, Hove & District added three Bristol Lodekka LDS6Gs to the fleet in 1959 with ECW sixty-seat bodies and fitted with a removable top deck roof. The first of the batch, No.1 (OPN801), is seen here. The FS Lodekkas had flat floors in the lower saloon. This example is fitted with a Cave-Browne-Cave heating system; hence the radiators either side of the destination screen in place of the normal radiator. (Roy Marshall/Southdown Enthusiasts' Club)

Further Lodekkas with removable top deck roofs were added to the Brighton, Hove & District fleet in 1962. These vehicles were of the FS6G model with standard ECW CO33/27R bodies. No.2041 (XPM 41) awaits passengers before operating the 17 service. (Southdown Enthusiasts' Club)

Passengers prefer to sit in the lower-deck of this Provincial No.56 (EHO 868), a Park Royal Guy Arab converted to open-top for the Gosport and Stokes Bay route. (C. Warren/Southdown Enthusiasts' Club)

A later convert to open-top, this Peoples Provincial Bus Co., a former Southdown Motor Services vehicle, numbered 201 (ROR 158B), is a fully fronted Northern Counties Leyland Titan PD3/4, and has been photographed at the Esplanade Fareham. (Geoff Mills)

In National Bus Co. days Southdown Motor Services took delivery of 594-603 (TNJ 994-9S/ TPN 100-103S) Bristol VRTSL3/6LXBs with ECW seventy-seat bodies, with the option to convert to open-top. These were unusual in having dual-doors. One of the batch, 598, was new in 1978 and is seen here in the then standard NBC livery of green and white relief. (Philip C. Miles collection)

In 1999 Brighton & Hove purchased two convertible Dennis Trident 2s, numbered 819 and 820 (T819/20 RFG). These modern double-deck buses have East Lancs Lolyne CO47/31F bodies. No.819 is seen here, named *Max Miller.* (Philip C. Miles collection)

En route to Devil's Dyke is Brighton & Hove 617 (GX03 SSZ), new in 2003. It is a Scania N94UD Omnidekka and carries an East Lancs CO47/32F body. It is also equipped to carry one wheelchair. 617 is named *Douglas Reeve.* This photograph shows the new modern image of open-top double-deck buses. (Philip C. Miles collection)

In 1964/65 Southdown Motor Services purchased numbers 400-429 Leyland Titan PD3/4s with Northern Counties fully fronted convertible open-top sixty-nine-seat bodies. One of the batch, seen here, is 419 (419 DCD) on the 197 service to Beachy Head. (Surfleet collection/ Southdown Enthusiasts' Club)

This attractive half cab was operated by Brighton Corporation Transport. No.32 (LUF 132F), a 1968 Leyland Titan PD3/4 with Metro Cammell H39/30F bodywork, was converted to an open-top bus along with numbers 33-35, after Brighton Borough Transport took over the open-top service 17 and the Round Brighton Tour from Southdown Motor Services in 1979. (W.J. Haynes/Southdown Enthusiasts' Club)

Few operators who ran trolleybuses and open-top buses converted trolleybuses to open-tops. However, Bournemouth Corporation Transport did. Originally numbered 157 (BRU 8), this 1936 Sunbeam MS2 with a Park Royal six-wheel body was converted in May 1958 and renumbered 400. This particular vehicle served for nearly thirty years with Bournemouth Transport. (Surfleet negative collection/Southdown Enthusiasts' Club)

Bournemouth was always popular with holidaymakers in years gone by. This fully fronted Leyland TD5 originally had a Metro Cammell Weymann forty-eight-seat dual-doorway body fitted with a sliding roof when new in 1939 to Bournemouth Corporation Transport as No.10. It was converted to diesel engine by Leyland in 1953 and converted to open-top in 1958. (L.W. Rowe/Southdown Enthusiasts' Club)

In 1965 Bournemouth Corporation Transport purchased twenty Daimler Fleetline CRG6LXs with Weymann bodies. Numbers 180-189 had convertible open-top H43/31F bodies. These buses were all named after counties in England. With a busy load of passengers, No.187 (CRU 187C), later named *Durham*, is seen here just before setting off for the coastal service to Hengistbury Head via Boscombe Pier. (Surfleet negative collection/Southdown Enthusiasts' Club)

The year 2002 saw the centenary of Bournemouth Corporation Transport. To commemorate this occasion No.431 (HJ02 HFB) was painted in a special gold and blue livery and lettered accordingly. 431 is one of three Volvo B7TLs with East Lancs Vyking convertible open-top seventy-six-seat bodies, and is seen here on service 12 to Christchurch. (Philip C. Miles collection)

Seen in the new mainly red livery is Wilts & Dorset 410 (HF05 GGU), a Volvo B7TL with an East Lancs Myllennium Vyking CO49/29F body, new in 2005. It is photographed passing Transdev Yellow Buses 474 a Dennis Dart SLF with an East Lancs B37F body, new in 1997. (Philip C. Miles collection)

The conductor collects fares from passengers on the upper-deck on service 25 bound for Hayling Ferry. English Electric bodywork was used on this Portsmouth Corporation 1935 Leyland Titan TD4 No.7, which was converted to open-top along with another three of the batch between 1953 and 1955, by which time these vehicles were already twenty years old. (Geoff Mills)

A recent vehicle to be converted to open-top is Portsmouth fleet No.249 (ERV 249D), a 1966 Leyland Atlantean PDR1/1 with a Metro Cammell O43/33F body. No.249 is seen here in Pompey, passing a traditional English meal advertisement. (Geoff Mills)

Southern Vectis 900 (GP 6244) is a 1931 AEC Regent which originally had a Tillings open staircase H27/25R body. It received its present BH & D body, which incorporated some of the original parts, in 1946. The cab entrance was not fitted with a cab door. New to Brighton, Hove & District as their No.6244, it was purchased by Southern Vectis in 1955 and entered service for the 1956 summer season painted in Tilling cream and green livery. (Eric Surfleet/ Southdown Enthusiasts' Club)

Another acquired open-top bus once operated by Southern Vectis is 908 (FLJ 538), a 1940 Bristol K5G with an ECW L27/26R body. New to Hants & Dorset as their TD761, it was renumbered 1086 in 1950. In 1954 a new highbridge ECW (KSW style) CO32/28R 8ft-wide body was fitted, with the option to convert to open-top. It was stolen in 1960 and driven under a low railway bridge at Fareham Station. The roof was damaged beyond repair, so it became a permanently open-topped bus. Southern Vectis acquired this bus in 1964. 908 is photographed here at Ryde, on the 42 service from Yarmouth to Alum Bay. (Geoff Mills)

In the smart Tilling cream livery with green bonnet, this 1940 Bristol K5G has an ECW fifty-six-seat body. No.703 (DDL 50) was converted to open-top in the winter of 1958/59. (Steve White)

Southern Vectis 501 (MDL 952) is a 1956 Bristol Lodekka LD6G with an ECW sixty-seat body. It was one of six similar vehicles delivered that year. Between 1973 and 1975 all six were converted to open-top, with 501 being converted in 1973 and renumbered OT2. It was again renumbered in 1984 as 501. In 1994 it received this smart Tilling cream livery with green bandings and wings. By then this bus was nearly forty years old. (Steve White)

Photographed in the smart leaf green and white livery, this Southern Vectis OT5 (MDL 955), a 1956 Bristol Lodekka LD6G with an ECW 33/27R body, was formerly No. 545. It was converted to open-top status in 1975, withdrawn in 1978, then returned back to Southern Vectis in 1993 and renumbered 500. (Steve White)

Southern Vectis acquired this 1977 Bristol VRTSL3/6LXB from Hants & Dorset Motor Services in 1979. No.506 (UFX 858S) carries a convertible open-top seventy-four-seat ECW body, and is seen here in standard National Bus Co. green and white. (Steve White)

Westbrook Travel was operating GTA 51N on an open-top service between Sandown and Ryde using this ex-Western National 1081, a Bristol VRTSL6G. It carries a standard National Bus Co. ECW 43/32F body. (Steve White)

Devon General was one of the few operators to purchase new convertible open-top buses in the 1960s. Devon General purchased nine buses, which became known as the 'Sea Dog' class. Each bus was named after a famous seafarer. No.932 (932 GTA), seen here, is a 1961 Leyland Atlantean with a Metro Cammell CO44/31F body. 932 is named *Earl Howe*. Note the conductor stood next to the driver in the days before one-man operations. (Photo by S.J. Butler/Southdown Enthusiasts' Club)

Opposite above: Seen in bright orange and yellow livery, this Southern Vectis 743 (K743 ODL), a 1993 Leyland Olympian ON2R50C13Z4, has a partially open-top seventy-four-seat Northern Counties body. Note the notice in the front upper-deck window which reads 'We accept Euro notes'. (Steve White)

Opposite below: The beautiful English Rivera around the Torbay area is always popular with holidaymakers and open-top buses. Devon General 507 (507 RUO) is named *Prince Regent*. New to the company in 1964, it is an AEC Regent MkV with a forward entrance Willowbrook O39/30F body. Few operators choose the forward entrance Regent MkV, Bridgemaster or Renown for open-top buses. (Geoff Mills)

River Link is the trading name of Dart Pleasure Craft. Here in Devon, visitors can travel on boats, steam trains and open-top buses on a round trip using a day ticket. The ticket allows passengers to travel on the railway from Paignton to Kingswear, then the Kingswear Dartmouth cross-river passenger ferry to Dartmouth-Totnes, an eleven-mile river cruise followed by a Totnes to Paignton open-top bus ride. In 2006 the price for this trip was only £14.50 for an adult. One of the open-top buses used was No. 3 (WTU 467W), a 1980 Bristol VRT/SL3 6LXB with an ECW O43/31F body. It was acquired from Arriva Cymru in 2002. (Steve White)

Repainted into First livery, No. 555 (ATA 555L) is a Bristol VRTSL2-6LX with an ECW converted O43/32F body, and was new to Devon General in 1973 as fleet No. 555. (Steve White)

3

SOUTH-WEST ENGLAND
AND WALES

Bristol Omnibus Co. began operating its Weston-super-Mare open-top bus service in 1950. Three AEC Regents, newly purchased between 1934 and '36, were offered as part of the take-over of Cheltenham District Traction Co. These three vehicles were converted to open-top and repainted in a cream livery with two green bands, one below the lower-deck and the other above the lower-deck windows. The route was numbered 152 and operated between the Old Pier, Grand Pier and the Sanitorium. Four Bristol Ks dating from 1939 were converted to open-top and entered service on the 152 route between 1951 and '53 replacing the AEC Regents. These Bristols continued to operate the Weston-super-Mare open-top service until 1961. Four convertible Bristol Lodekka FS6Gs numbered 8576-8579 took over the service, now numbered 103, and extended it to Uphill. In 1973 Bristol Omnibus purchased three Lodekka LD6Bs from Crosville Motor Services and converted them to open-top. Two of these received all-cream livery with the new NBC fleet name in red down the side, along with the town coat of arms. The third vehicle was given a special livery to celebrate Bristol's 600th Charter Anniversary. This Lodekka operated a tour of the city, continuing up until 1980. In 1976 six Lodekkas with open-tops were repainted into liveries of the former tramway companies. Each vehicle also depicted a painting on its side for each town or city, which it was well known for. The vehicles repainted were:

7900. *Western Challenger* dark blue (Concorde)
8576. *Western Pioneer* brown (Gloster Gladiator aircraft)
8577. *Western Conqueror* crimson (GWR City of Truro engine)
8578. *Western Grandeur* light blue (Royal Crescent, Bath)
8579. *Western Superior* dark blue (Clifton Suspension Bridge)
8590. *Western Splendour* bright red (Weston-super-Mare Grand Pier)
8581. *Western Winner* red (Cheltenham Gold Cup)

In 1980 buses on the open-top service in Weston-super-Mare were converted to have their engines at the rear, using ex-Hants and Dorset Leyland Atlanteans with Roe bodies, which were new to King Alfred in 1967. Further rear-engined buses entered the fleet in 1981. These were: a Leyland Atlantean with Weymann bodywork dating from 1963, from Maidstone & District, and ex-Midland Red Daimler Fleetlines with Alexander bodies. Bristol introduced a new open-top service operating between Burnham-on-Sea and Brean Down as service 137. The service to Sand Bay was renumbered 100, whilst in 1982 the Burnham-on-Sea service was extended to Weston-super-Mare seafront as service 151. Vehicles on this route were given a new image, painted white with a light blue skirt with the lettering 'Coast Rider'. Bristol purchased two Bristol VRTs in 1983. These had ECW convertible open-top bodies and were new in 1977 to Hants & Dorset, passing to Southern Vectis. A new open-top service was introduced to Bath in 1983 on a city tour. Badgerline, who took over the Weston-super-Mare routes, repainted the older open-top buses in a striking livery of yellow and blue and the newer buses in the then standard Badgerline livery. A cute feature on the latter was that the badger logo had sunglasses and a bucket and spade. Badgerline also took over the Bath tour and operated it in conjunction with Guide Friday. Another operator to utilise the Bath tour was Bath Bus Co., who operated a variety of vehicles including ex-London Transport AEC Routemasters. First Somerset & Avon is the present operator, running the Bath tour and also the open-top service in Weston-super-Mare, whilst First Hampshire & Dorset operate the 501 service between Weymouth and Portland. The open-top service 308 operating between Falmouth and Pendennis is operated by First Devon and Cornwall.

Western Greyhound operate ex-London Transport Routemasters in the Newquay area on service 500.Quantock Motor Services of Taunton purchased East Lancs Scania Omnidekkas in 2005 for service 300, operating between Minehead and Ilfacombe via Lynton, Lynmouth and Combe Martin.

The Isles of Scilly, twenty-nine miles west of Lands End, operate an ex-Morecambe & Heysham Transport AEC Regent III of 1949 vintage with bodywork by Park Royal. This is used on open-top tours of the small island of St Mary's. This service was operated by Jim Nichols in 2001. Another open-top bus used on this route is former Lancaster Corporation Transport Leyland Titan PD2/41 with an East Lancs body, ex-No.128. Glyn Lucas operates this vehicle, and it is painted red with London Transport fleet names.

Crosville Motor Services operate an open-top service between Prestatyn and Pensarn operating via Rhyl as service M87. In the post-war years ex-Brighton, Hove and District AEC Regents and the more unusual Leyland LT3s were converted to open-top thirty-six-seat bodies, until these delightful vehicles were replaced by Bristol Lodekka LDs. Another open-top service operated by Crosville was the M88 from Rhyl Promenade via the Botanical Gardens to Maes Gwilym. During the National Bus Co. days vehicles were painted in an all-white livery. After Crosville Motor Services was split up into two in 1986, in 1987 the management bought Crosville Wales. These open-top buses were used on a service between Conwy and Talacre as service 100, although in later years the service only operated between Prestatyn and Llandudno via Rhyl. Buses used on this service were given a new image: buses were painted in bright green, orange and white livery with a large dragon's head in red. The service was marketed as the 'Happy Dragon' service, and ran every thirty minutes. A new service was opened between Chester and Wrexham as service 1. These buses were also painted in the Happy Dragon livery.

Arriva now operates the open-top service along the coast of North Wales, operating between Rhyl and Prestatyn. Arriva also operate the Sherpa service S1/S2 either from Llandudno or Betws-Y-Coed to Pen-Y-Pass, passing some of the most breathtaking scenery of Snowdonia National Park. KMP of Llanberis also operates the Snowdonia Sherpa service S1 between Llanberis and Pen-Y-Pass using ex-Plymouth Citybus East Lancs-bodied Leyland Atlanteans in an all-blue livery. Cardiff City Transport for a number of years operated a tour of the city, whilst South Wales Transport operated open-top buses in the Swansea area. In 1977 South Wales Transport repainted No.500, an ex-Eastern National Bristol KSW5G, in all-silver livery for the Queens Silver Jubilee. Another bus operator who once operated open-top buses in South Wales was Thomas Bros (Port Talbot) Ltd, operating a service between Aberavon Beach and the market to Sandfields housing estate, at one time using ex-Brighton, Hove & District Bristol Ks.

Western National Omnibus Co. operated No.3822 (GHT 122), a Bristol K which was in later years converted to open-top. (Roy Marshall/Southdown Enthusiasts' Club)

A later Western National vehicle to be converted to open-top was No.1935 (VDV 752), a Bristol LDL6G with an ECW 037/33R body, new in 1957. After the conversion it was given the name of *Admiral Boscawen* and repainted in a reverse livery of the old Tilling cream and green livery. (Steve White)

In 1976 Bristol Omnibus Co. repainted a number of Bristol Lodekkas in special liveries representing the colours of the old tram system which once operated in Bristol, Bath, Cheltenham, Swindon and Weston-super-Mare. No.8579 (869 NHT) is a 1964 FS6G with an ECW seventy-seat open-top body. Repainted into the old Bristol tram livery, it is named *Western Superior* and depicts a painting of the Clifton Suspension Bridge. (Steve White)

Also repainted in a special livery was No.8580 (626 HFM), named *Western Splendour* and depicting the Weston-super-Mare Grand Pier on the side. This vehicle is a LD6G model new to Crosville Motor Services in 1959 as their DLB977. It was acquired by Bristol in 1973. (Steve White)

Bristol Omnibus Co. purchased two second-hand buses from Midland Red in 1967. These Daimler Fleetline CRG6Ls with Alexander bodywork were then converted to open-top. Photographed on the service to Sand Bay is 8606 (LHA 615F). These vehicles, with their Alexander bodies, were an unusual choice for Bristol. (Steve White)

Photographed back in the National Bus Co. days and carrying a Weston and Wells fleet name, this is Bristol Omnibus 8609 (A809 THW), new in 1984. It is a Leyland Olympian ONLXB/1R with a Roe convertible CO47/29F body, and carries a mainly cream livery. Note the position of the NBC double N emblem. (Steve White)

Seen in the mainly green livery of Badgerline, this open-top 8619 (JHW 114P), a 1976 Bristol VRT/SL3 6LXB with an ECW O43/29F body, was new to Bristol Omnibus Co. Here, passengers board 8619 for the return journey to Weston-super-Mare. (Philip C. Miles collection)

Featuring a large badger on the side is Badgerline No.8614 (A814 THW), new in 1984. Badgerline operated a number of former Bristol Omnibus Co.'s Leyland Olympian ONLX/Rs with Roe convertible to open-top seventy-six-seat bodies. These vehicles were mainly based at Weston-super-Mare for the seafront service between the town and Sands Bay. (Steve White)

Southern National 934 (VDV 134S) is seen with the new company after privatisation. It was new to Devon General in 1977, passing to Southern National in 1983. Several of these Bristol VRT/SL3 6LXBs were delivered during the National Bus Co. era, and had ECW convertible seventy-four-seat bodies. (Steve White)

Above: This former Brighton, Hove & District Bristol K5G with an ECW H30/26R body, new in 1940, was converted to open-top in 1951 for use in the Brighton area. It was later sold to Thomas Bros of Port Talbot, who named her *Afan Belle*. She is seen here in July 1965. (Geoff Mills)

Left: Crosville Motor Services DLG950 (286 HFM) is a Bristol Lodekka LD6G with a semi-open-top ECW 33/27RD body. (Steve White)

Opposite above: Crosville Motor Services DLG814 (XFM 226) is a Bristol Lodekka LD6G with an ECW O33/27RD body, new in 1955. DLG814 is seen here at Colwyn Bay in the smart mainly cream livery. (Steve White)

Opposite below: Photographed in an all-National Bus Co. white livery, this Crosville Motor Services DFG72 (882 VFM) is one of a batch taken into stock in 1961/62. DFG72 is a later Bristol Lodekka FSF6G model with an ECW converted 34/26F body. This vehicle is operating the busy Prestatyn–Rhyl–Towyn–Pensarn route. (Steve White)

In 1989 South Wales Transport celebrated its 75th anniversary. No.931 (RTH 931S), a Bristol VRTSL3-501 with an ECW seventy-four-seat convertible open-top body, was repainted into the old South Wales Transport maroon and cream livery. (Steve White)

Cardiff City Transport repainted No.85 (JKG 485F) into Cardiff Corporation Tramways livery in 1983. It is a 1967 Daimler Fleetline CRG6LX/30 with a converted MCW seventy-five-seat body. It was converted to open-top in 1980. (Philip C. Miles collection)

Cardiff City Transport purchased a large number of Bristol VRTSL3/6LXBs with unusual Alexander AL H43/31F bodies between 1978 and 1980. Two of the batch, 359 and 360, were convertible open-top vehicles, as seen here by No.360 (WTG 360T). (Steve White)

Crosville Wales/Cymru operated an open-top service between Talacre, Prestatyn, Rhyl, Llandudno and Conway, giving beautiful views from the upper-deck. Vehicles operating on this service are branded as the 'Happy Dragon' and have a large dragon in red on a yellow background. Seen on this service is DFG27 (308 PFM), a 1960 Bristol Lodekka FS6G with an ECW converted sixty-seat body. (Steve White)

Also in the Crosville Wales/Cymru fleet is DVG528 (DCA 528X), a 1981 Bristol VRTSL3/6LXB with an ECW seventy-four-seat body. It was converted to open-top for the Happy Dragon 100 service. Like the Lodekka, this bus is painted green, white and yellow. (Steve White)

This Arriva Cymru No.3995 (G35 HKY), a 1990 Scania N113DRB with converted to open-top Northern Counties O47/33F bodywork, can be seen on the Sherpa S2 service operating between Betws-Y-Coed and Pen-Y-Pass in the beautiful Snowdonia National Park in North Wales, photographed at Pen-Y-Pass during the poor summer of 2007. (Philip C. Miles collection)

4

THE EAST COAST

The Coastal & Country Coach Co. now operate an open-top tour of the small historic town of Whitby serving the town and the abbey. An ex-West Yorkshire PTE Leyland Olympian operates the tour which, in its entirety, takes about an hour, although passengers may alight and board the bus at certain points. At only £4.00 per adult it is well worth it.

In Scarborough, the United Automobile Services hired a Southdown Motor Services Leyland Titan PD3/4 No.3215 (415 DCD) during the summer of 1979 for the seafront service, using a fully-fronted Northern Counties open-top. The bus retained the NBC green livery whilst at Scarborough, but received United fleet names, operating between the Spa complex on the South Bay along the promenade to Corner Café (now demolished) on the North Bay, later converting a number of ex-Scottish Bus Group Bristol VRTs, which were also converted to open-top. Another conversion was No.4278 (PHN 178L), a Bristol RELL6G with ECW bodywork painted in the old olive green and cream livery.

United was divided up in preparation for privatisation in 1986. The Scarborough and Pickering operations were transferred to a subsidiary of East Yorkshire Motor Services Ltd and given the fleet name of Scarborough & District. Scarborough & District have operated a wide variety of open-top buses on this service over the last twenty years, including Atlanteans with ECW dual-doorway bodywork acquired from Northern in 1986, Bristol VRTs from Yorkshire Traction and Trent, and numerous Leyland Atlanteans acquired from other operators. A number of former Devon General convertible open-top Bristol VRTs were also operated, having been acquired in 1992, whilst a number of ex-London Transport AEC Routemasters were also converted to open-top. After de-regulation of bus services a number of other operators competed on the 109 service. These included Wallace Arnold, using ex-Greater Manchester Leyland Atllanteans, Applebys, who operated a Bristol Lodekka FS6G (869 NHT) along with ex-Southend-on-Sea Daimler Fleetline, and Shoreline Suncruises, who operated Daimler or Leyland Fleetlines acquired from West Midlands PTE, Thamesdown Transport and Grimsby-Cleethorpes Transport.

Only two operators now use this service: Scarborough & District and Shoreline Suncruises, both of whom continue to operate a variety of vehicles, with Shoreline now operating ex-West Midlands Travel Metrobuses, whilst Scarborough & District are using a Volvo B10M Citybus with a Northern Counties eighty-two-seat body. For the 2007 season three Volvo Citybuses were enlisted from Finglands. A short-lived open-top service 108 ran from North Bay (Corner Café) to the town centre using a cut down Mercedes Benz L608D with Reeve Burgess O20F bodywork, new in 1986. In the summer of 1978 East Yorkshire Motor Services hired Western National No.1935 – a 1957 Bristol Lodekka LDL6G with an ECW open-top seventy-seat body. East Yorkshire Motor Services operated 1935, given the fleet No.102, on a service in Bridlington. After the trials with 1935, East Yorkshire Motor Services converted two ex-Tynemouth & District Daimler Fleetlines with Alexander H43/30F bodies, new in 1965, converted to open-tops during the winter of 1978/79 and painted in special liveries devised by local schoolchildren. 900 (AFT 783C) was named *Belvedere Star* whilst 901 (AFT 784C) was named *Sewerby Star.* Further convertible open-top buses were purchased between 1982 and '83 from Western National Omnibus Co. when three 1961 Leyland Atlantean PDR1/1s with Metro Cammell seventy-five-seat bodywork were acquired. These became 902 (926 GTA), named *Flamborough Star,* 903 (931 GTA) *Bridlington Star* and 904 (932 GTA) *Belvedere Star.*

After privatisation East Yorkshire Motor Services purchased a number of Leyland Atlanteans and converted them to open-tops for the Bridlington service between Belvedere and Sewerby. This service was discontinued in the early 1990s. Across the River Humber in Lincolnshire is Cleethorpes. Grimsby-Cleethorpes Transport operated an open-top service using a 1960 AEC Bridgemaster with a Park Royal rear entrance body, converted to open-top in 1974. After this bus was withdrawn two Daimler and Leyland Fleetlines were converted to open-top for the service between Cleethorpes Pier with its many holiday bungalows and Pleasure Island. Stagecoach now operated the service using ex-West Midlands Travel Metrobuses.

In the popular seaside resort of Skegness, Lincolnshire Road Car acquired two Bristol Lodekka FS6Gs with ECW bodies from Southdown Motor Services. New to Brighton, Hove and District, they were converted to open-top for a service between Richmond Drive, the seafront and Winthorpe Avenue. The two FS6Gs were numbered 2350 and 2351 and named *Lincolnshire Imp* and *Lincolnshire Poacher* respectively. They were both painted in an all-white livery. Three Leyland Atlantean PDR1/1s with MCW convertible open-top seventy-five-seat bodies were purchased from Devon General in 1983/84 for the service, and numbered 2351, 2353 and 2354. After privatisation Bristol VRTs and second-hand Leyland Atlanteans purchased from Greater Manchester Transport and the Borough of Blackburn Transport operated the service. By this time, during the summer of 2006, the service operated to Butlins and Chapel St Leonards. However, now owned by Stagecoach, only one open-top service remains, No.99, operating between the bus station and Chapel St Leonards by ex-Travel West Midlands Metrobuses. The Metrobuses have been painted into a new livery and the service, now renumbered 3, terminates at Ingoldmells. Further down the east coast is Great Yarmouth, once served by Great Yarmouth Corporation Transport, who operated an AEC Regent with an English Electric body. This became an open-top bus in 1953, following an accident. Later the open-top service was operated by Cobholm Hire Services, trading as Caroline Seagull, using ex-Edinburgh Leyland Atlanteans. The service was known as the 'The Seaside Special', stopping at Seashore Camp, Waterways, Britannia Pier, Marina Centre, Wellington Pier and the Pleasure Beach. Along the Essex coastline, Eastern National was once the main operator of open-top buses, running services in Clacton and Southend-on-Sea. Eastern National has operated open-top buses in the area since 1950, when four ex-Brighton, Hove & District AEC Regents were decapitated.

By 1966 Bristol KSW6Gs acquired from Westcliffe-on-Sea Motor Services were used. After privatisation Bristol VRTs were converted to open-top. In Southend the seafront service 67/68 was operated jointly between Southend Transport and Eastern National. The service ran every fifteen minutes, passing the famous one-and-a-half-mile pier. Southend Corporation Transport purchased a number of Daimler CWA6s from Eastern National in 1955, which were later rebuilt as open-top buses. These buses were ex-Westcliff-on-Sea Motors. Some were new to Birmingham City Transport. Further buses converted to open-top included Leyland PD3/6s with attractive Massey bodywork, converted in 1970/71, and in 1980 four Daimler Fleetline CRL6/33s with Northern Counties dual-doorways were converted.

New to the West Yorkshire PTE in 1981 as their No.5002 (UWW 2X) is this Leyland Olympian ONLXB/1R with a Roe H47/29F body. It is seen converted to open-top and operated by Coastal & Country Coach Co. on the Whitby Town Tour. (Philip C. Miles collection)

Go Ahead Northern operated an open-top service between Tynemouth and Whitley Bay. No.3285 (RCN 111W), a 1974 Leyland Atlantean AN68/1R with a Park Royal body, seen here, has been converted to an open-top seventy-seven-seater. (Philip C. Miles collection)

Opposite above: Busways repainted their 1227 (SVK627G), a Leyland Atlantean PDR1A/1R with an Alexander converted to open-top seventy-four-seat body, into the old Economic livery. It wears route branding on the upper-deck advert panels for the service operating between South Shields and Sunderland. (Philip C. Miles collection)

Opposite below: Northumbria Motor Services also operated an open-top service, running between Whitley Bay and North Shields. Seen here on that route is their 555 (YCU 961T), a 1979 Bristol VRT/SL3-6LXB with a converted to open-top seventy-four-seat body, which came from the United fleet in 1986. (Philip C. Miles collection)

1. Now preserved, this Portsmouth Corporation Transport 124 (RV 6367) was new to the corporation in 1935. A Leyland Titan TD4 with a converted to open-top English Electric fifty-four-seat body, this photograph was taken at a bus rally in 1975. (Philip C. Miles collection)

2. This 1965 Daimler Fleetline with a Weymann convertible to open-top seventy-four-seat body was new in this year to Bournemouth Corporation Transport. It was acquired by London Transport in 1977 and repainted into standard red livery and numbered DMO6. (Philip C. Miles collection)

3. East Yorkshire Motor Services purchased a number of London Transport AEC Routemasters with Park Royal H36/28R bodies, some of which were later converted to open-top. Seen here at Scarborough is 816 (CUV 210C), carrying the Scarborough & District fleet name. It was formerly RM2210. (Philip C. Miles collection)

4. In 1978 Lincolnshire Road Car purchased this Bristol Lodekka FS6G with an ECW convertible to open-top sixty-seat body. It was named the *Lincoln Imp* and numbered 2350 (XPM 41). It was new in 1962 to Souhdown Motor Services. This bus is now preserved. (Philip C. Miles collection)

5. Vehicles operated by Crosville Cymru/Wales on the open-top service between LLandudno and Prestatyn were branded 'Happy Dragon'. One such vehicle is DDL195 (JTD 395P), an ex-Southend Corporation/Transport Daimler Fleetline with a converted to open-top Northern Counties seventy-eight-seat body. It was new to that undertaking in 1976 and acquired by Crosville Cymru in 1993. (Philip C. Miles collection)

6. Chester City Transport operated a tour of the city on behalf of Guide Friday, although the vehicles used remained in standard livery. Photographed here, No.90 (KFM 190T), a Daimler Fleetline with a converted to open-top Northern Counties seventy-two-seat body, was new in 1978. (Philip C. Miles collection)

7. Scarborough & District operated this Volvo Citybus with a converted to open-top Alexander body. It was numbered 897 (G128 PGK) in the fleet. This photograph was taken at the South Bay terminus, and shows a newly converted and freshly repainted bus, although it is not carrying any fleet name. (Philip C. Miles collection)

8. Bournemouth Corporation Transport purchased ten Daimler Fleetlines with convertible to open-top Weymann seventy-four-seat bodies in 1965. These were all named after counties in England. No.181 (CFRU 181C), seen here, is named *Yorkshire*. (Philip C. Miles collection)

9. New in 1967 to Colchester Borough Transport, No.48 (YWC 648F) is a Leyland Atlantean with a Massey seventy-four-seat body. It was later converted to open-top for a tour of Colchester. (Philip C. Miles collection)

10. This is Road Car 1318 (DBV 198W), a 1980 Leyland Atlantean AN68/1R with a converted to open-top East Lancs seventy-eight-seat body, seen here in Guide Friday livery. Visible behind the bus is the beautiful Lincoln Cathedral. This bus was new to Hynburn Borough Transport, passing to Road Car in 1992. (Philip C. Miles collection)

11. MTL Merseyside operated No.1612 (GKA 37N), a Leyland Atlantean AN68/1R with a converted to open-top Alexander AL seventy-five-seat body. New in 1974, it is seen here working the popular tour of the town in August 1996, in the old Southport livery. (Philip C. Miles collection)

12. Photographed in an all-white livery with the large 'NATIONAL' fleet name is PFN 879. New to East Kent in 1959, and converted to open-top in 1972, this fully fronted AEC Regent V with a Park Royal body was acquired by National Travel South East in 1976 and used as a publicity vehicle. (Philip C. Miles collection)

13. Alpine was operating JPL 105K, a former London Country Bus Services Leyland Atlantean PDR1A/1 with converted to open-top seventy-two-seat dual-door Park Royal body. It was used on the Guide Friday tour of Llandudno and Conwy. This photograph was taken on the Llandudno promenade. (Philip C. Miles collection)

14. In the smart blue and white livery of Cambus Ltd, No. 60 (JAH 552D) was new to Eastern Counties in 1966. This Bristol Lodekka FLF6G with its ECW seventy-seat body was converted to open-top for use on special events. (Philip C. Miles collection)

15. Photographed in the old bus garage at Weston-super-Mare, this is Badgerline 8604 (612 UKM), a 1960 Leyland Atlantean PDR1/1 with a Weymann converted to open-top seventy-seven-seat body. It was new to Maidstone & District as their 5612. (Philip C. Miles collection)

16. Southend Transport was using 915 (JTD 395P) in August 1992 on the popular open-top service. It is a Daimler Fleetline with a Northern Counties eighty-seat dual-door body, new in 1976. (Philip C. Miles collection)

17. After Eastern National was sold off from the National Bus Co. buses were painted in a nearly all-yellow livery. Seen in this bright, modern livery, open-top 3027 (NPU 974M) is a Bristol VRTSL6G with an ECW seventy-seat body, new in 1974. (Philip C. Miles collection)

18. Photographed at the beautiful Bowness, this Stagecoach Cumberland 2075 (XRR 175S) is a 1980 Bristol VRTSL3/6LXB with an ECW seventy-four-seat body, converted to open-top. It is painted in a slightly different livery from other Stagecoach buses. (Philip C. Miles collection)

19. Greater Manchester Transport converted 7077 (WBN 955L), a 1972 Leyland Atlantean with a Park Royal seventy-five-seat body, into an open-top. Open-tops are often used for private hire, rather than on tours of the city or town. They are useful, for example, when a football team wins a promotion or a cup; the bus can be used by the team to show their trophy off to the crowd. (Philip C. Miles collection)

20. Carrying a good load is Crosville Cymru/Wales DVL429 (RLG 429V), a Bristol VRTSL3/501 with converted to open-top ECW seventy-four-seat body, is seen here at the new bus station at Rhyl, on the Happy Dragon 100 service. The route gives excellent views of the North Wales coastline. (Philip C. Miles collection)

21. Photographed at Sandtoft trolleybus museum, Busways 1218 (KBB 118D) was new in 1966. It is a Leyland Atlantean PDR1/1R with a MCW seventy-eight-seat body, which was cut down to open-top. It was often used on the seafront service between South Shields and Sunderland. (Philip C. Miles collection)

22. During the National Bus Co. era, new Bristol VRTs with ECWs convertible to open-top were purchased for use with several operators. One such NBC operator who took delivery of several of these buses was Devon General. Seen in the smart red and white livery is No.941 (VDV 141S), named *Illustrious*. Naming buses is a long tradition with Devon General, dating back to 1919. (Philip C. Miles collection)

23. Carrying the Mainline fleet name is No.287 (SWB 287L), a Leyland Atlantean AN68/1R with an Alexander converted to open-top seventy-four-seat body. (Philip C. Miles collection)

24. United Automobile converted No.4278 (PHN 178L), a Bristol RELL6G with an ECW fifty-seat body, into open-top. It was used on the Scarborough seafront service. It is photographed after East Yorkshire Motor Services took over the Scarborough and Pickering area in 1986. (Philip C. Miles collection)

25. Road Car No.1304 (LJA 642P) is seen at the old bus station in Skegness. This Leyland Atlantean AN68/1R with a Northern Counties converted to open-top seventy-five-seat body was acquired from GM Buses in 1988. (Philip C. Miles collection)

26. Seen here is Arriva's Merseyside No.1449 (GKA 449L), a Leyland Atlantean AN68/1R with a cut down to open-top seventy-five-seat Alexander AL body, having just dropped the passengers off outside Pontins holiday camp. (Philip C. Miles collection)

27. Photographed whilst working the Oxford tour for Guide Friday, GTO 335N, a former City of Nottingham Transport Leyland Atlantean AN68/1R with an East Lancs seventy-eight-seat dual-door body, was later converted by Guide Friday to open-top for sightseeing work. (Philip C. Miles collection)

28. London Sightseeing Tours Ltd once operated this former London Transport Daimler Fleetline. Its Park Royal seventy-five-seat dual-door body was converted to open-top for the tour of London, which lasted anything between one and two hours. (Philip C. Miles collection)

29. Emerging from the bus garage at Weston-super-Mare for the service to Sands Bay is Badgerline 8610 (A810 THW). New to Bristol Omnibuses in 1984, this Leyland Olympian ONLXB/1R has a Roe convertible open-top body. Passengers can only guess were this bus is heading, as the destination board gives no information. (Philip C. Miles collection)

30. Flyde Borough Transport, trading as Blue Buses, was operating an open-top bus service along Blackpool's promenade in this 1996 photograph. Seen operating on this service is No.53 (WRH 294J), which was new to Kingston-upon-Hull City Transport as their 294 in 1970. A Leyland Atlantean PDR1A/1 with a Roe seventy-one-seat body, it was altered to a partially open-top by Flyde Borough Council. (Philip C. Miles collection)

31. New to Southport Corporation Transport as their No.51, this Leyland Titan PD2/40 with a Weymann sixty-four-seat body passed to Merseyside PTE in 1974, carrying fleet No.0651 (CWM 151C), is seen here converted to open-top. (Philip C. Miles collection)

32. Operating on the Lakeland Experience in the Lake District is Stagecoach Cumberland 2036 (UWV 612S). This 1978 Bristol VRT/SL3/6LXB with an ECW body was new to Southdown Motor Services. (Philip C. Miles collection)

Scarborough with a castle, sandy beaches, and, of course, open-top buses. United Automobile operated an open-top service along the promenade from Spa to North Bay and Corner Cafe. Seen here is 636 (NGM176G), a 1969 Bristol VRT/SL6G with a converted to open-top seventy-five-seat ECW body. It was one of the vehicles transferred from Scottish bus companies in 1973, in this instance from Eastern Scottish. (Philip C. Miles collection)

Applebys operated this ex-Southend Borough Transport Daimler Fleetline CRL6 with a Northern Counties open-top 49/31D body. It was new as Southend's 387 in 1976. It is leaving the Corner Café terminus at Scarborough. (David Longbottom)

Another operator running the open-top seafront service at Scarborough is Shoreline Suncruisers. This former West Midlands PTE Leyland Fleetline with a MCW seventy-six-seat body which was converted to open-top has been photographed on the promenade. (David Longbottom)

One of the open-top buses transferred from United Automobile in 1986 was this Bristol VRT/ SL2 /6G with an ECW converted seventy-four-seat body. New in 1974 as No.658 (BHN 758N), it can be seen here at the southern end of the route at the Spa. The Grand Hotel is visible in the background. (Philip C. Miles collection)

Scarborough & District Motor Services 838 (VDV 138S) is photographed with the large bow tie on the front. This Bristol VRT/SL3/6LXB with a convertible ECW seventy-four-seat body was new in 1977 to Devon General. It was acquired by S&DMS in 1992. (Philip C. Miles collection)

A much travelled bus is Scarborough & District 619 (WBN 959L). It was new to Greater Manchester Transport as their 7080 in 1973. This Leyland Atlantean AN68A/1R with a cut down open-top Park Royal seventy-five-seat body was passed to Hardwicks of Scarborough who used it on the seafront service. It then passed to Scarborough & District in 1988. (Philip C. Miles collection)

Another vehicle which came with the United fleet is East Yorkshire Motor Services No.600 (PHN 178L). It was numbered 4278 and converted to open-top by United for the seafront service at Scarborough. This Bristol RELL6G with an ECW fifty-seat body is photographed operating a guided tour of the town. It carries the name *Bridlington* and is also named *Sea Princess*. (Philip C. Miles collection)

A number of AEC Routemasters were purchased by East Yorkshire Motor Services in the late 1980s and early 1990s. Several were later converted to open-top, as shown here by 812 (ALM 65B) for use on the open-top seafront service at Scarborough. It was new to London Transport as their RM2065. (Philip C. Miles collection)

Scarborough & District 890 (AVK 177V) is a Leyland Atlantean AN68A/2R with an Alexander AL converted open-top body. 890 waits for passengers before setting off for the Corner Café in North Bay. (Philip C. Miles collection)

This MCW Metrobus DR101/17 with a MCW dual-doorway body, seen here in October 2007, was new to London Buses as their M1227 (B227 WUL). It is now operated by Shoreline Suncruises of Scarborough. Passengers alight from the centre doors. (Philip C. Miles collection)

Few operators have chosen to operate mini buses as open-top buses. However, Scarborough & District converted No.407 (C407 VVN) to operate an open-top mini bus service between the Corner Café and the town centre. No.407 was new to United Automobile Co. in 1986, passing to Scarborough & District in the same year. It is a Mercedes Benz L608D with a Reeve Burgess open-top twenty-seat body. (Philip C. Miles collection)

Scarborough & District now operate No.897 (897 EYX), formerly registered G128 PGK. It is a Volvo B10M Citybus-50 with a Northern Counties converted open-top eighty-two-seat dual-doorway body, seen here before setting for North Bay. (Philip C. Miles collection)

The open-top service in Bridlington used to be operated by East Yorkshire Motor Services between the bus station and Sewerby. Photographed in the National Bus Co. days, 904 (932 GTA) was named *Belvedere Star*. It is a former Western National Leyland Atlantean PDR1/1 with a Metro-Cammell CO44/31F body, new in 1961 as Western National 932. (Malcolm King)

East Yorkshire Motor Services converted No.900 (AFT 783C) to open-top for use on the Bridlington seafront service. It was new to Tynemouth Transport in 1965, passing to East Yorkshire in 1972. No.900 is a Daimler Fleetline CRG6LX with an Alexander O43/31F body. It is seen here in the old bus station at Bridlington. (Philip C. Miles collection)

New in 1960, this AEC Bridgemaster was once owned by Grimsby-Cleethorpes Transport. Its Park Royal body was cut down to open-top in 1974. No.133 (NJV 995) is now preserved and is seen alongside an East Yorkshire Motor Services Bridgemaster. (Philip C. Miles collection)

Stagecoach Grimsby-Cleethorpes can be seen here in the old white and striped livery of the time. No.113 (MBE 613R) is a 1976 Leyland Fleetline with a converted open-top Roe O45/29D body, photographed at the pier at Cleethorpes before beginning its run via the promenade to the holiday camps on service 17. (Philip C. Miles collection)

Serving Grimsby Cleethorpes, Stagecoach now operates 14667 (H667 BNL), an ex-Stagecoach Busways vehicle, which was converted to open-top for the promenade service. No.14667 is a 1990 Leyland Olympian ON2R50C13Z4 with a Northern Counties Palatine seventy-seven-seat body. (Philip C. Miles collection)

An unidentified company operated this former Devon General Leyland Atlantean PDR1/1 with a Metro Cammell convertible to open-top seventy-five-seat body. When new in 1961, it was numbered 927 (927 GTA) and named *Sir Martin Frobisher*. It is seen here in later years working at Ingoldmells. (Philip C. Miles collection)

Heading back to Skegness along the Pleasure Beach is Road Car 1971 (HWJ924W), a Bristol VRT/SL3-6LXB with a converted to open-top seventy-four-seat ECW body, new to Yorkshire Traction in 1980, passing to Road Car in 1988. (Philip C. Miles collection)

Few passengers wish to travel on Road Car No.1314 (UBV 84L), seen here on Skegness promenade. New in 1972 to the Borough of Blackburn Transport as their No.84, this Leyland Atlantean AN68/1R has an East Lancs converted open-top seventy-five-seat body. (Philip C. Miles collection)

Road Car operated this partially open-top Leyland Atlantean AN68A/1R with a Northern Counties seventy-five-seat body, new to Greater Manchester Buses in 1976, and acquired by Road Car in 1988. No.1306 (LJA 622P) is seen here at Skegness. (David Longbottom)

Opposite above: Also seen at Skegness is a similar Leyland Atlantean AN68A/1R with a Northern Counties body, which was also acquired from Greater Manchester Buses. However, 1304 (LJA 642P) was converted to full open guise. In the background is open-top No.1317 on service 92 to Ingoldmells. (David Longbottom)

Opposite below: Stagecoach in Lincolnshire now operates the open-top service between Skegness and Ingoldmells, passing Butlins camp. The service is operated by ex-West Midlands Travel Metrobus Mk2s, as can be seen here by No.15952 (WOI 3002). The livery represents the sand, sea and sun. The jolly fisherman can also be seen to the top left of the front wheel. No.15952 is photographed at Ingoldmells during the poor summer of 2008. (Philip C. Miles collection)

Southend Corporation Transport 246, an ex-Eastern National Omnibus Daimler CWA6 with a converted to open-top Duple fifty-six-seat body. It was new to Eastern National in 1944, in whose fleet it was No.1198, before being purchased by Southend Corporation in 1955 and converted in 1956. (Philip C. Miles collection)

Opposite above: HX 2980 is an AEC Regent I with an ECW fifty-six-seat body. New in 1932 as a demonstrator, it was acquired by Westcliff-on-Sea Motors who converted it to open-top. It is seen working service 19A operating between Southend, Esplanade and Westcliff-on-Sea. Note that early converted open-top buses did not have a windshield at the front of the upper-deck. (Philip C. Miles collection)

Opposite below: New in 1953 was Eastern National O.C. 2382 (WNO 478), a Bristol KSW5G with an ECW H33/28R body. It was converted to open-top in 1966, giving several more years of life to this vehicle. The upper-deck front windows have been retained and used as a windbreak. This vehicle carries a mainly cream livery with a green bonnet and green relief between the decks. (Essex Bus Enthusiasts' Group)

Westcliff-on-Sea Motors operated this Dennis Lance with a BHD body. NJ 5976 was one of six buses acquired from Brighton, Hove & District. It was later converted to open-top and had an AEC radiator fitted. (Essex Bus Enthusiasts' Group)

Opposite above: The ultimate open-top bus is the half cab. This smart, well-turned-out Bristol K with an ECW body was converted to open-top while working for Eastern National Omnibus. Nevertheless, few passengers seem to want to view the sights from the open-top! (Philip C. Miles collection)

Opposite below: Southend Transport No. 314 (PHJ 953), new in 1958, was one of the batch 311-316 purchased in that year. They were Leyland Titan PD3/6s with Massey L35/33R bodies. During the winter of 1970/71 numbers 311-314 were converted to open-top for the seafront service. (Essex Bus Enthusiasts' Club)

This Eastern Counties OT1 operated a seaside special between Sherringham, Cromer and Overstrand. Eastern Counties acquired this vehicle from Western National in 1979, in whose fleet it was No.1935. It is a Bristol Lodekka LDL6G with an ECW seventy-seat converted open-top body, new in 1957. (Steve White)

Eastern National converted this 1974 Bristol VRTSL6G with an ECW body to open-top. No.3027 (XPU 974M) is seen in the yellow and green livery adapted after privatisation. Eastern National operated open-top services in the Clacton-on-Sea and Southend areas. (Steve White)

5

NORTH-WEST ENGLAND AND SCOTLAND

The west coast of England boasts several holiday resorts. These are Southport, Lytham St Annes, Blackpool, Fleetwood and Morecambe, all of which have operated open-top buses at one time or another. Thousands of people in the 1920s up until the 1960s travelled by charabanc, bus or train from the industrial cities of Liverpool, Manchester, Bradford, Leeds and Sheffield to sample the fresh air, and no doubt travel on an open-top bus. The small seaside resort of Southport (once in Lancashire and now in Merseyside after the corporation was taken over by the Merseyside PTE in April 1974) was the first local authority to re-introduce open-top buses, operating a service from the pier on a circular tour of the town. Four 1934 Leyland TD3s with English Electric bodies, numbers 42-45, were converted to open-top between 1951 and 1952. In 1957 these buses were renumbered 142-145. For a number of years ex-Ministry of Defence four-wheel-drive Bedford QLs with lorry chassis were used. These were numbered 1-4 and entered service in 1946. No.1 had bodywork by Southport Corporation Transport. The other three had twenty-three or twenty-four-seat bodies built by Rimmer, Harrison & Sutherland. A further eight of these unusual vehicles arrived in 1947. These unique vehicles operated to Ainsdale beach – the terminus being on the beach itself – operating between 1947 and 1953. Numbers 13-18 were originally operated as rear-wheel drive and used solely on the circular tour, although numbers 15, 17 and 18 were converted to four-wheel drive for the Ainsdale Beach service and were the property of Southport Publicity and Attractions Department. The town service continued to be operated by Leyland Titans converted to open-top. These were 1947 Leyland PD2/3s with Leyland bodies converted to open-top between 1962 and 1963, and three Leyland Tiger PS2s with Burlingham B35F bodies, new in 1950 to Ribble Motor Services, converted to open-top in 1963/64 and numbered 10-12. After Merseyside PTE took over the council bus service, it was operated by front entrance Weymann-bodied Leyland Titan PD2/40s and later by Leyland Atlanteans. MTL later took over the services operated by Merseytravel. They were then transferred to Arriva, who now operate the open-top service in Southport. Buses operating the Southport open-top service through the town are still painted in the old Southport livery, whilst those running from the Monument to Pontins are painted in standard Arriva livery. Further up the west coast, Lytham St Annes also operated an open-top bus service along the promenade using fully fronted Leyland Titans. In later years, after the Fylde Council Transport was privatised, were operating open-top Leyland Atlanteans acquired from Kingston-upon-Hull City Transport, in competition with Blackpool Transport on the promenade service in Blackpool. Neighbouring Blackpool, better known today for its trams, was once an enthusiastic user of open-top buses, using both single-deck and double-deck buses. In 1932 the corporation purchased four Leyland Lion LT5s with Burlingham B30D bodies. These saloons had sunshine

Southport Corporation Transport 14, a 1934 Leyland Titan TD3 with an EEC H25/26R body, was, in late 1950 to early 1951, converted to open-top, having its seating increased at the same time to 30/26, using wooden seats in the upstairs from a withdrawn wartime Daimler. It is seen here in August 1962, renumbered 142. (Geoff Mills)

roofs fitted, which, when sunny, could be opened. The single-deck buses used by Blackpool Corporation Transport were unusual: the first single-deck buses used by Blackpool Corporation were twelve Leyland Lion PLSC3s with Roe OB33C bodies. The chassis were new in 1928, with thirty-five-seat fully enclosed bodies, fitted in 1937 and remaining in service until 1954, twenty-six years old. In 1935, under the then General Manager Walter Luffs, the council took delivery of six unusual Leyland Tiger LT7s with Burlingham OB34C bodies. These were the 'Gondola' runabouts – the bus version of open tram boats 225-236 – numbered 114-119. These Gondola buses must have looked magnificent on the roads of Blackpool, and saw service until 1956. These were followed in 1939 by six petrol-engined Leyland Cheetahs, again with Burlingham central entrance bodies seating thirty-four, although they were built to a less orthodox design and numbered 19-24, and were not sold until 1961. Three Leyland Titan TD5s numbered 26-28, new in 1940, were converted to open-tops in 1959, but only saw three or four years service as open-top buses before they were withdrawn. These had Burlingham central entrance/exit bodies and were used on a North Shore Circular service.

Another seaside resort is Morecambe, once a popular resort with its long promenade and beautiful views across Morecambe Bay. Morecambe was another early user of open-top double-deck buses, running them from the Battery to Happy Mount Park, operated by Morecambe Corporation Transport. The later Morecambe & Heysham Corporation in 1938 purchased new AEC Regent double-deck buses with Park Royal highbridge bodies. These bodies were unusual in that the central part of the roof could be rolled back. Two of these vehicles, numbers 25 and 49, were converted to open-top status in 1962 for the promenade service. Further buses were converted to open to,: numbers 62, 64 and 65, and a further three vehicles were converted in 1968 when 60, 61 and 63 became open-top buses. In 1969 No.58 was also converted. This vehicle differed from the previous vehicles as this one only had its roof taken off, leaving the windows all around the bus intact. After local government reorganisation in 1974, further AEC Regents were converted to open-top, now under the control of Lancaster City Council. Ex-Lancaster City Council bus No.201 (201 YTE), a Leyland Titan PD2/37 with East Lancashire body, was converted to open-top in 1976, with numbers 202 and 203 becoming open-top the following year. No.201 once again only had the roof removed, whilst similar vehicles 202 and 203 became open-top buses. One-man-operated buses began to take over the route in 1980 using ex-Greater Manchester PTE Leyland Atlanteans, new to Salford City Transport in 1965. During the Jubilee Year of 1977 the open-top double-deck buses 58, 60, 62 and 65 were named *The Queen Mother*, *Prince Edward*, *Princess Anne* and *Prince Andrew* respectively, whilst 201-203 were named *Duke of Edinburgh*, *Queen Elizabeth II* and *Prince of Wales*. All were renamed during 1978/79, with character names being taken from *Snow White and the Seven Dwarfs*, becoming *Snow White*, *Dopey*, *Happy*, *Sleepy*, *Sneezey*, *Doc* and *Grumpy* respectively. An additional open-top No.88 was named *Bashful*. Numbers 201-203 were renamed yet again in 1980, becoming *Ullswater*, *Wast Water* and *Tarn Hows*. The Leyland Atlanteans 227, 228 and 230 became *Thirlmere*, *Buttermere* and *Windermere*. In

1981 the Leyland Atlanteans 218, 227 and 230 became *Lady Diana*, *Prince Charles* and *St Paul*. Atlantean 228 was painted with an all-over advertisement for Sealink Isle of Man. Further second-hand Leyland Atlaneans were acquired from Blackburn Borough Transport with East Lancs H45/31F bodies, new in 1972, purchased by Lancaster City Council in 1985. A number of these were also converted to open-top and given names.

In the beautiful Lake District Stagecoach Cumberland operate two open-top routes: the 599 operating between Bowness and Grasmere, branded as 'the Lakeland experience', and route 79, operating between Keswick to the village of Seatoller. This service is branded as 'the Borrowdale Bus'. On both routes the buses were painted in a smart green and cream livery, although this was discontinued in 2006 when the vehicles were repainted in corporate liveries. The Mountain Goat Holidays & Tours operated a short-lived open-top service in the Grasmere and Bowness area using an ex-Midland Red Daimler Fleetline. It was branded 'the Lakeland Shuttle'. The service later passed to Guide Friday.

The majority of open-top buses operating in Scotland were tours of the towns and

Southport Corporation Transport purchased a number of Bedford QL's four-wheel-drive chassis, ex-army wagons in 1946/7. These strange-looking machines had bodywork by Southport Corporation Transport for No.1 and by Rimmer, Harrison and Sutherland of Stockport for numbers 2-4 and 11-18. These vehicles operated between Ainsdale Beach and Southport Pier. The bus shown here is No.1 (EWM 680) and carried the original Southport Corporation Transport body. (Geoff Mills)

In 1947 Southport Corporation transport purchased No.85 (FFY 402), one of seven such vehicles. These were Leyland Titan PD2/3s with attractive Leyland bodywork, seating fifty-six. Six of the batch was converted to open-top in 1962 for the circular town service. Note the fare; 2s (10p). (Ribble Enthusiasts' Group)

cities. In Edinburgh Lothian Buses operated a tour of the city. Another open-top service was the Majestic Tour to the Royal Yacht *Britannia*. Mac Tours also operated in Edinburgh. In Glasgow the open-top tour was operated by Greater Glasgow PTE, and the vehicles operated in the old Glasgow Corporation Transport livery. First Glasgow now operates the service. P&D Travel also operate an open-top tour of Glasgow. Stagecoach Western converted OSJ 636R, an Alexander-bodied Leyland Leopard, for use on the Isle of Arran tour. Later, Stagecoach Western repainted No.11083, a Leyland Titan, into the pre-war black and white livery to celebrate the SMT 75th anniversary, and this vehicle currently operates on the Isle of Arran tour. In Aberdeen, First Aberdeen operates the open-top tour, whilst open tours are also operated in Greenock, Inverness, the Isle of Arran, Isle of Bute and Oban.

This open-top round-the-town bus service was popular with many holidaymakers visiting Southport. In 1963 Southport Corporation Transport purchased three Leyland Tiger PS2/5s with Burlingham B35F bodywork, new in 1950. No.10 (CRN 990), new as Ribbles 2790, was converted to open-top and entered service in this form in 1963. It is photographed here two years later waiting for passengers. (Geoff Mills)

MTL Southport repainted a number of open-top buses in the old Southport Corporation livery. One such vehicle is 1524 (GKA524M), new in 1974. It is a Leyland Atlantean AN68/1R with an Alexander AL seventy-five-seat body converted to open-top. 1524 is seen here working the Southport circular rather than the town tour. (Philip C. Miles collection)

Arriva Merseyside operated this Leyland Atlantean AN68/1R with an Alexander seventy-five-seat converted to open-top body. New in 1974, it is seen here in Arriva corporate livery on its way to Pontins holiday camp. (Philip C. Miles collection)

Blackpool Corporation Transport used the original 1928 Leyland Lion PLSC3 bodies. In 1937 they were replaced with Roe open-top thirty-three-seat central entrance bodies. One of the batch, No.61 (FR 9144), is photographed here after receiving its new open-top body. This vehicle was not withdrawn from service until 1954, by then twenty-six years old. (Huddersfield Passenger Transport Group)

In 1935 Blackpool Corporation Transport took delivery of six 'Gondola' runabout Leyland Tiger LT7s. These had H.V. Burlingham thirty-four-seat central entrance bodies. These impressive single-deck open-top buses were based on the design of the 'boat' trams 225-236. One of six numbered 114-119,118 (FV 6128) is seen here heading towards Central Station. These vehicles must have looked superb on the streets of Blackpool. (Huddersfield Passenger Transport Group)

Opposite above: Blackpool Corporation Transport purchased the last of its open-top single-deck buses in 1939: six Leyland Cheetahs with Burlingham thirty-four-seat central entrance/exit bodies. These were numbered 19-24 (BFR 360-365), and remained in service until withdrawn in 1961. No.19 is seen here. (Huddersfield Passenger Transport Group)

Opposite below: In 1940 Blackpool Corporation Transport purchased this Leyland Titan TD5, with its Blackpool specified full-fronted body which conceals the radiators. The bodywork was done by H.V. Burlingham and was H25/23C. No.28 (BFR 369) was converted to open-top in 1959 and is seen here on an illumination tour. It was withdrawn the following year. (Huddersfield Passenger Transport Group)

This 1938 AEC Regent with a Park Royal body was new to Morecambe & Heysham Transport as No.49. (DTB 68) It was converted to open-top in 1962 for the Morecambe seafront service between Happy Mount Park and the Battery. (Philip C. Miles collection)

Opposite above: A moving castle! Morecambe & Heysham Transport No.25 (DTB64) is a 1938 AEC Regent I with a Park Royal body, converted to open-top for the Morecambe seafront service to New Heysham Head. The view for the front passengers must have been very poor. (Geoff Mills)

Opposite below: Heading towards the Battery and Heysham village is Morecambe & Heysham Corporation Transport No.60 (KTF589), an AEC MkIII with a Park Royal converted to open-top fifty-nine-seat body. Note the old Hillman Imp car on the right. (Philip C. Miles collection)

Formerly in the Morecambe & Heysham Corporation fleet as their No.62, this AEC Regent MkIII with a Park Royal converted to open-top fifty-nine-seat body, now numbered 591 (KTF589) of the Lancaster City Council fleet, is named *Happy* and is seen here carrying a portrait of the dwarf of that name. (Geoff Mills)

Opposite above: New to Salford Corporation as No.227 (DBA 227C), this vehicle passed to the south-east Lancashire-based North East Cheshire Transport, becoming No.3073. It was one of a batch of Leyland Atlantean PDR1/1 with Metro Cammell H43/33F bodies purchased in 1964/65. Some of this batch were sold to Lancaster City Council. Seen here in its new disguise as No.227 (again) and converted to open-top, this bus was named *Thirlmere* in 1980, then in 1981 renamed *Prince Charles*. (Geoff Mills)

Opposite below: Lancaster City Council purchased this Leyland Atlantean AN68/1R with an East Lancs H45/31F body from Blackburn Borough Transport in 1985. It was new to Blackburn in 1972. Lancaster City Council converted it to a partially open-top, leaving the upper-deck windows in place. Numbered 87 (UBV87L), it was named *Ben Nevis* and is seen here in Heysham village. (Philp C. Miles collection)

Also acquired from Blackburn Borough Transport, this Lancaster City Council Leyland Atlantean, numbered 84, has an East Lancs H45/31F body. This bus, however, was converted to fully open-top, and is seen here on Morecambe Promenade, going by the name *Helvellyn*. (Geoff Mills)

Opposite above: Seen here on Blackpool promenade, the ex-Hull Corporation Transport vehicle No.54 (ARH 307K) was operated by Fylde Council Transport, trading as Blue Buses. It is a 1972 Leyland Atlantean PDR1/1 with a Roe seventy-two-seat single-door body. The upper-deck was cut down to partially open-top. (Philip C. Miles collection)

Opposite below: Stagecoach Cumberland painted a number of open-top buses in an attractive green and cream livery for use on services in the Lake District. One such vehicle in this livery is No.2129 (VRN 829Y), an ex-Stagecoach Ribble Leyland Olympian ONLXB1/1R with a converted open-top seventy-seven-seat body. (David Longbottom)

Eastern Scottish operated OT1 (GCS 246), a 1955 Bristol Lodekka LD6G with an ECW converted open-top 31/25RD body. New to Western Scottish Omnibuses Ltd, OT1 is photographed here in Edinburgh, outside the former C&A store. Note the cameraman on the upper-deck. (Geoff Mills)

Opposite above: Mac Tours of Edinburgh was using No.15 (869 NHT), a former Bristol Omnibuses Co. Bristol Lodekka FS6G with a convertible open-top ECW body. (Steve White)

Opposite below: Painted in a bright yellow livery, there is no mistaking the fleet name of this operator. Clydeside Scottish converted this Daimler Fleetline CRG6LX with an Alexander H44/31F body to an open-top. Numbered R2 (SMS 402H), it formerly belonged to Northern Scottish Omnibuses, although it was originally new to Alexander (Midland). (Philip C. Miles collection)

In an all-over advertisement livery for a well-known alcoholic drink, A949 SUL, a Metrobus DR101 with a MCW converted to partial open-top body, has been photographed in George Square, Glasgow. New to London Buses as their M949, it is now operated by A. Pringle (trading as Scotguide) Clydebank for city sightseeing. (Geoff Mills)

6

IN TOWNS AND CITIES

Few bus operators use open-top buses on regular bus services in towns and cities, although many of our historic places like Bath, Bristol, Chester, Lincoln and York, to name a few, operate open-top buses to convey tourists. Many operators run these sightseeing tours, giving the tourists an opportunity to see the historic sites from the comfort of a seat. They can get on and off the bus as they please, exploring one site and then catching the next bus to the next site. Or if they wish, they can just do a circular trip. Like most historical towns, York is a hive of bus operators using open-top buses for tours of the city. These have included York Pullman and Lothian Transport. In Bath, Bath Bus Co. once operated its own city tours using a variety of vehicles including ex-London Transport AEC Routemasters. In Lincoln Road Car also operated a tour of the city.

West Yorkshire Road Car operated the open-top bus service in York. One vehicle converted for this work was No.1956 (FWT 956J), a 1970 Bristol VRTSL6G with an ECW seventy-seat body. It is seen with the Viewmaster fleet name, photographed in Rougier Street in October 1988. (Philip C. Miles collection)

Other open-top buses are used as special event buses, such as conveying football clubs, rugby clubs etc. who have won cups or have been promoted to a new division. They can proudly go through the streets of their hometown or city on open-top buses showing off their prize cup to supporters. In some places the open-top bus is used to promote a new store or special event. Eastern National once used a Bristol KSW as a Santa Special from its Clacton depot. The upper-deck was rebuilt to include the upper-deck of a house and roof, with Father Christmas at the front of the bus waving to the children. Another use for the open-top bus in town and cities is for tree lopping: cutting the branches of trees on busy roads and overgrown rural routes. Many buses, having spent many years on regular bus routes, finish their days cut down to open-tops for this essential duty. During the months the open-top bus is not used in service on the promenades of the holiday resorts, it may also be used as a learner vehicle.

A number of operators over the years have operated the city tour of York. Lothian Transport was an unusual choice to operate this service. No.928 (DSF 928M), named *Saxon Star*, is a 1974 Leyland Atlantean AN68/1R with an Alexander converted seventy-eight-seat body. One of York's many old buildings can be seen in the background. (David Longbottom)

Displaying on the side of the bus 'See all the sights from York's first open-top service', West Yorkshire Road Car's 3954 (DWU 839H) is a 1970 Bristol VRT SL6G with a converted open-top seventy-seat ECW body. (John H. Meredith)

Chester City Transport converetd this Leyland Fleetline with a Northern Counties seventy-two-seat body to a partially open-top. New in 1978, No.92 (KFM192T) is seen here in its new disguise, working the Chester Tour. (Philip C. Miles collection)

Opposite above: Also working the Chester Tour is Chester City Transport No.98 (SDM98V), a 1980 Leyland Fleetline with a converted to fully open-top Northern Counties seventy-two-seat body. (Philip C. Miles collection)

Opposite below: Another operator to use open-top buses on the city tour of York was York Pullman. This service was owned by Kingston-upon-Hull City Transport for a while using ex-Hull Leyland Atlanteans. One such vehicle is 194 (DRH 321L), ex-Hull Corporation 321, a 1972 Leyland Atlantean AN68/1R with a cut down partially open-topped Roe 43/29F body. (David Longbottom)

Alder Valley 896 (LFS 296F) is one of three ex-Scottish Bus Group Bristol VRTs in the 1974 exchange scheme for Bristol Lodekka FLFs. Transferred to Southdown Motor Services and passed to Alder Valley in 1980, it became an open-top in 1983. No.896 is a VRTLL-6LX with an ECW seventy-four-seat body. (Steve White)

An unusual vehicle for Cleveland Transit to purchase was this former Southdown Motor Services Leyland Titan PD3/4 with a Northern Counties convertible to open-top H39/31F body. New in 1964, it passed to Cleveland Transit in 1988 as their No.500(PRX 189B). (Geoff Mills)

Northern Bus operating in South Yorkshire ran this former Crosville Bristol Lodekka LD6G. Built with a removable open-top ECW sixty-seat body, this vehicle was new in 1959. Northern Rose purchased 627 HFM from Dunn-Line of Nottingham in 1991. (Steve White)

SELNEC converetd this 1951 Leyland Titan PD2/1 with a Leyland forty-eight-seat body into an open-top vehicle. It was used as a tree-lopper, but re-licensed as an open-top p.s.v. vehicle for summer tours and private hire. It was new to Stockport Corporation as their 295 (EDB549), becoming SELNEC's 2995. (Philip C. Miles collection)

ECW bus work was chosen by a few municipals for other chassis besides the standard Bristol VRT chassis. Thamesdown Transport purchased a number of Daimler Fleetlines with ECW bodywork in the late 1970s and early 1980s. One such vehicle is 175 (KMW 175P). New in 1976, it was converted to open-top in 1985 for private hire work. (Steve White)

First Somerset & Avon No.9550 (L650 SUU), a Northern Counties seventy-six-seat converted to open-top Volvo Olympian YN2RC16ZS, is seen here on the Bath tour awaiting passengers. (Steve White)

The Bristol K lives on! Badgerline operated this delightful old timer Bristol K5G of 1941 vintage with an Eastern Coach works fifty-nine-seat body converted to open-top. It came from Bristol Omnibuses in 1990. 8583 is named *Prince Bladud* and operated the Bath tour. (Steve White)

Another Bristol, but not as old as the Bristol K, is First 39943 (VDV 143S). A 1978 Bristol VRTSL3/6LXB with an ECW convertible to open-top 43/31F body, this vehicle was new to Western National and operated with the Devon General fleet name whilst operating open-top services in the Torquay area. It was photographed whilst operating the Bath tour. (Steve White)

This former London Transport AEC Routemaster was converted to open-top for the Bath tour. New to London Transport as RM1783 (which it still carries), Bath Bus Co. now operates the Bath tour on behalf of City Sightseeing. (Steve White)

Windorsian at one time operated this former London Transport DMS1304 (MLH 304L). A Daimler Fleetline with a converted to open-top body, it was used on the Round Windsor Sightseeing Tour. Arthur Road is the setting for MLH 304L. (Geoff Mills)

Photographed at the Great Central Railway, 4518 (A134 SMA) is an ECW-bodied converted open-top Leyland Olympian. Owned by Arriva, it was operated by Leicester Promotions on a 'Discover Leicester Tour'. (Geoff Mills)

The guide seen on the left of the top deck gives a running commentary to passengers on board Road Car No.1318 (DBV 198W), a 1980 Leyland Atlantean AN68B/1R with a converted open-top East Lancs 45/31F body. New to Hynburn Transport in 1980, it passed to Road Car in 1992. (David Longbottom)

Thamesdown Transport ex-183 (OHR 183R), a 1977 Leyland Fleetline with an unusual ECW body, served for many years on busy local routes carrying thousands of passengers. It is seen here in later life cut down to an open-top, and is now used on route maintenance, cutting the branches of trees on double-deck bus routes. (Steve White)

Photographed outside the East Yorkshire Motor Services bus depot on Anlaby Road in Hull, 8833, a former Devon General Bristol VRT with ECW convertible to open-top bodywork, was acquired by EYMS and used to carry the many tourists at Scarborough on the 109 service. It is seen here in 2007 painted all-yellow and with additional hazard warning lights fitted. It is now used as a tree-lopping vehicle. (Philip C. Miles collection)

7

GUIDE FRIDAY AND CITY SIGHTSEEING TOURS

Roger Thompson started Guide Friday. His first tour was in William Shakespeare's birthplace of Stratford-upon-Avon. With the many tourists visiting this town, this was an ideal location. In 1976 Thompson operated a twenty-seat Bedford coach for a tour of the town and surrounding area, although at this time it was not known as Guide Friday, operating instead under the name of Stratford-go-Round. The tour lasted half a day, taking in most if not all the attractions in and around the area. Passengers at this time, however, could not get off the coach and explore the sites. With this in mind, Thompson purchased his first bus in 1978: an ex-Leicester City Transport Leyland Titan PD3, registered 264 ERY, which he had converted to open-top, allowing passengers to disembark at key points. A professional also provided live commentary in English. It was soon realised, however, that the rear entrance bus was unsuitable for this kind of work: the driver was in a cab and could not take the fares or watch for passengers getting on and off the bus. So ex-Nottingham City Transport Leyland Atlanteans and Daimler Fleetlines were purchased and converted to open-top. The driver was now responsible for taking the fares and keeping an eye on passengers boarding and alighting from the vehicle, leaving the guide to concentrate on giving commentary. It was also necessary to operate a frequent service, since visitors who alighted did not want to be waiting a long time for the next bus.

The business was a success, and Guide Friday began to expand to other cities and towns, including Cambridge, Bath, Edinburgh and York. The green and cream open-top buses were also to become a familiar sight in historical cities and towns like Windsor, Glasgow, Salisbury, Canterbury, Lincoln, Chester and Portsmouth, as well as in various seaside resorts including Brighton and Llandudno. In some cities and towns an agreement was made with the local bus operators who would supply and maintain vehicles, and even provide extra staff. In Lincoln this was undertaken by Road Car, whilst in Chester the vehicles were owned by Chester City Transport.

One feature of Guide Friday's tour was that once you paid your fare you could travel around a city or town getting on and off as many times as you wished in the course of a day. The ticket also afforded you discounts to many of the sites, and if you retained the bottom part of the ticket this would allow you a discount on another Guide Friday tour.

Photographed outside York Railway Station, Guide Friday DWU 839H, a Bristol VRTSL2/6LX with a converted open-top ECW seventy-seat body, was new to the West Yorkshire Road Car as their 3954 in 1970. The York walls are just visible on the left behind a First single-deck bus. (Steve White)

Also, whilst all Guide Friday tours had live commentary in English, a recorded commentary in several other languages was available on some of the buses. On these vehicles the passengers wore headphones, which were provided on boarding the bus. The passenger could then switch to the recorded foreign language commentary of their choice. Such buses were easily identified by the many different national flags on the front of the bus.

From mid-2000 a livery change took place.

Over the years various types of buses have been operated by Guide Friday, including former Maidstone & District AEC Regals with Beadle bodywork, and ex-Bristol Omnibus Co. Bristol K5Gs. Many former Nottingham City Transport buses have operated on tours throughout England. Ensign began operating open-top buses in 2001, the first of these in red livery. Services commenced in Cambridge, Blackpool, Stratford-upon-Avon, Newcastle, Colchester, Cardiff and Windsor, often in direct competition with Guide Friday. After a year of contest between the two operators, Ensign acquired the assets of Guide Friday in May 2002. City Sightseeing Tours repainted many former Guide Friday vehicles, and also purchased many other buses and painted these in a dominant all-red livery with a yellow stripe from the front windscreen going upwards to the second top window. City Sightseeing also purchased a few ex-London Buses Leyland Titans and Metrobuses, as well as some more modern buses from other fleets. The most recent being Volvo B7TLs with Spanish-built Ayats bodywork.

Like Guide Friday, City Sightseeing Tours have expanded all over England, Scotland and Wales, and these bright red buses are now a common sight in most cities and towns. During the winter of 2006 a surprise came when operations at Stratford-upon-Avon and Cambridge were acquired by Stagecoach. The depot at Stratford-upon-Avon soon gained the Stagecoach branding, whilst vehicles in the City Sightseeing fleet operated on hire to Stagecoach during February 2007. These hired vehicles ran with the legal name of Midland Red South on paper bills in the windows. A third City Sightseeing operation was taken over by Stagecoach in Newcastle and Gateshead, with the new service beginning on 31 March. Here Stagecoach used newly converted open-top Olympians.

The beginning: this was the first bus Guide Friday operated. Bought in 1978 and converted to open-top for its new role of sightseeing around Stratford-upon-Avon, 264 ERY, a 1963 Leyland Titan PD3A/1 with a Park Royal H41/33R body, was new to Leicester City Transport as their No.264. It was bought by Guide Friday in 1978. (Philip C. Miles collection)

An unusual vehicle for the Guide Friday fleet is HKL 826; an AEC Regal with a Beadle converted to open-top thirty-six-seat body. It was new to Maidstone & District in 1946, converted to an open-top in 1957, and passed to Guide Friday in 1989. (David Longbottom)

Opposite above: An ex-London Transport Daimler Fleetline with a converted to open-top Metro Cammell O44/31D body, this bus was new in 1972 as DMS1304. It is seen here working on the Brighton tour. Behind can be seen two Scania double-deck buses of the Brighton & Hove fleet. (David Longbottom)

Opposite below: Guide Friday operated GVO 715N, an ex-Nottingham City Transport Leyland Atlantean AN68/1R with an East Lancs body, converted to single door and open-top. It is photographed here on the Statford Tour, operating to and from Shakespeare's birthplace, Anne Hathaway's cottage and Mary Arden's house. The guide can be seen on the front upper-deck. (David Longbottom)

This ex-South Yorkshire PTE Leyland Atlantean AN8/1R with a converted to open-top Roe 45/29D body has been photographed at Cambridge Railway Station. DWJ 546V was new in 1979 as the PTEs 1740, passing to Guide Friday in 1991. (Geoff Mills)

Also photographed on the Cambridge tour, RFN 957G, a Daimler Fleetline CRG6LX with a Park Royal 39/31F body, was new to East Kent Road Car in 1969. Seen decapitated for its new role and carrying a full load of passengers, this photograph of RFN 957G was taken in Drummer Street. (Geoff Mills)

Originally in the Nottingham City Transport fleet is MAU 614P, this 1976 Leyland Atlantean AN68/1R with an East Lancs converted to open-top 047/33D body is seen here awaiting passengers before setting off on an Oxford tour. (David Longbottom)

Seen here in its new Guide Friday livery, A156 EPG, a Leyland Olympian ONTL11/1R with a Roe 043/29F body, has been converted to an open-top. It was new to Wilts & Dorset in 1983, passing to Guide Friday in 2000. A156 FPG is photographed on the Glasgow tour operated by Scotguide. (Philip C. Miles collection)

Operating on the Blackpool sightseeing tour, 217 (VRG 417T) A M.C.W. Metrobus has a partially converted open-top seventy-six-seat body. Formerly 0017 of the MTL fleet, it was new to London Buses in 1979. (Philip C. Miles collection)

City Sightseeing 397 (A697 SUL) is photographed here operating on the Bournemouth tour. It is a Metrobus with dual-doorway converted to open-top seventy-one-seat body, new to London Buses as their M897. (Philip C. Miles collection)

Bath Bus Co. operates the Bath tour on behalf of City Sightseeing. New to Bristol Omnibus Co. in 1976 as their 5079 (NFB 115R), this Bristol VRTSL3/6LXB with an ECW dual-door H43/27D body was purchased for use on Bristol city services. It later passed to Stringer of Pontefract, South Yorkshire, but is seen here after it was purchased by Bath Bus Co. in 1997 and converted to a partially open-top. (Steve White)

Hundreds of Bristol VRTs were purchased by National Bus Co. during the late 1970s and 1980s. Seen here in later years converted to open-top for the Bath tour, belonging to Bath Bus Co., BCL 213T, a Bristol VRTSL3/6LXB with a standard NBC/ECW H43/31F body, was purchased in 1997 from APT Rayleigh and converted to open-top status. (Steve White)

Operated by Lothian Buses on behalf of City Sightseeing Tours for the Edinburgh tour, 305
(E305 MSG) is a 1988 Leyland Olympian ONCL10/2RZ with an Alexander open-top 51/28F
body. This photograph was taken at Waverley Bridge. (Geoff Mills)

Seen in the High Street, Glasgow, A983 SYF, a former Go-Ahead London Metrobus DR101 with
a MCW 43/28D converted to partially open-top, is operated by A. Pringle, trading as Scotguide
of Clydebank. (Geoff Mills)

Bath Bus Co. operates vehicles in all-red livery on behalf of City Sightseeing. No.248 (N548 LHG) is an ex-London Buses Leyland Olympian with a Northern Counties partially converted open-top seventy-five-seat dual-doorway body. (Steve White)

Photographed on the Edinburgh tour, No.32 (W632 PSX), a Dennis Trident with a Plaxton President converted to open-top 51/26F body, was new to Lothian Buses in 2000. This photograph was taken in Hanover Street, Edinburgh. (Geoff Mills)

This ex-South Yorkshire PTE Metrobus is seen here at the Pier Head partway through a tour of Liverpool. New to PTE in 1980 as their No.457, DR102/3 has a partially converted open-top 046/27D body. (Geoff Mills)

Opposite above: Alpine Travel of Llandudno was operating A654 OCX, an ex-Yorkshire Traction No.654 Leyland Olympian ONLXB/1R with a converted to open-top ECW 45/32F body. It is photographed here awaiting passengers on Llandudno promenade during the summer of 2007. (Philip C. Miles collection)

Opposite below: City Sightseeing was using this Metrobus on their Stirling tour in 2006. Converted to a partially open-top, it was ideal if the weatehr changed for the worse. BYX189V is seen here on Goosecroft Road operating the Wallace Route Tour. (Geoff Mills)

City Sightseeing operated No.326 (WYV 26T), a Leyland Titan TNLXB2RRsp with a converted to open-top Park Royal sixty-six-seat dual-door body. New to London Buses as T26, it is photographed here on the Bristol tour. (Steve White)

From Wales to Scotland; this former City of Cardiff Leyland Olympian ONLXB/1R with a converted to open-top seventy-four-seat East Lancs body was new to Cardiff City Transport as their 514. It is seen here working some distance from its home on the Stirling Bruce route outside the Bannockburn Heritage Centre in 2006, being operated by A. Pringle, trading as Scotguide. (Geoff Mills)

New to Newport Transport as their No.41 (F41YHB) in 1989, this Scania N113DRB with an Alexander RH H47/31F body was converted to a partially open-top. It is seen here working the Newport tour on behalf of City Sightseeing. (Geoff Mills)

The newest buses in the City Sightseeing tours fleet are Volvo B7TLs with Spanish-built Ayats seventy-nine-seat partially open-top bodies. No.272 (EU05 VBG) is operated by Bath Bus Co. and is seen here operating in that city. (Steve White)

Other titles published by The History Press

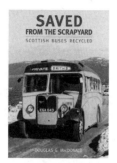

Saved From the Scrapyard: Scottish Buses Recycled
DOUGLAS G. MACDONALD

In his inimitable and humorous style, Douglas MacDonald looks at the changing bus scene in Scotland since the 1950s and the fascinating range of different tasks undertaken by the country's old buses, which include polling booths, showmen's transport, recovery trucks, car transporters, mobile canteens, mobile homes, and much more.

978 0 7524 3880 1

Hull's Transport
PHILIP C. MILES

This engaging book looks at the various forms of transport used in Hull from the 1880s to the present day. It includes a detailed look at Hull's bridges (including the Humber Bridge) as well as trams, ferries and trolleybuses. A fascinating read for anyone interested in both transport history and that of the area.

978 0 7524 4206 8

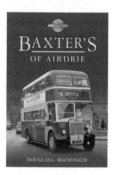

Baxter's of Airdrie
DOUGLAS G. MACDONALD

This book takes us on a tour of Baxter's operations, with images of the Airdrie-based company's fleet and its employees in both Airdrie and Coatbridge, and the surrounding outskirts. Using original photographs, combined with information and memories from the founder's grandson, MacDonald tells the story of what was once Scotland's largest independent bus operator.

978 0 7524 4229 7

The United Counties Story
ROBERT COOK and ANDREW SHOULER

This is the story of the United Counties Omnibus Co., once one of Britain's largest and most influential bus companies. Robert Cook and Andrew Shouler combine social and transport history as they narrate the memories of people who worked in the local bus industry and detail the vehicles employed by the bus operators of this once great national bus company.

978 0 7524 3199 4

Visit our website and discover thousands of other History Press books.
www.thehistorypress.co.uk